Martin Luther

Luther disguised as Knight George in a painting by Lucas Cranach, 1521–22.
Source: Art Resource, N.Y.

Paul W. Robinson
Concordia Seminary

Martin Luther
A Life Reformed

THE LIBRARY OF WORLD BIOGRAPHY

Edited by Peter N. Stearns

Longman
Boston Columbus Indianapolis New York San Francisco Upper Saddle River
Amsterdam Cape Town Dubai London Madrid Milan Munich Paris Montreal Toronto
Delhi Mexico City Sao Paulo Sydney Hong Kong Seoul Singapore Taipei Tokyo

Editorial Director: Leah Jewell
Executive Editor: Charles Cavaliere
Editorial Assistant: Lauren Aylward
Director of Marketing: Brandy Dawson
Project Manager: Renata Butera
Creative Art Director: Jayne Conte
Cover Designer: Karen Salzbach
Cover illustration/Photo: #113 Portrait of Martin Luther (1483-1546) (oil on panel) by
    Cranach, Lucas, the Elder (1472-1553) Germanisches Nationalmuseum, Nuremberg,
    Germany / THE BRIDGEMAN ART LIBRARY.
Full-Service Project Management: Saraswathi Muralidhar/GGS Higher Education
    Resources, A Division of PreMedia Global Inc.
Composition: GGS Higher Education Resources, A Division of PreMedia Global Inc.
Printer/Binder: Courier-Stoughton
Text Font: 10/12 Sabon

Library of Congress Cataloging-in-Publication Data

Robinson, Paul W.
    Martin Luther–: a life reformed / Paul W. Robinson.
        p. cm. — (Library of world biography series)
    Includes bibliographical references and index.
    ISBN-13: 978-0-205-60492-0
    ISBN-10: 0-205-60492-7
    1. Luther, Martin, 1483-1546.   2. Reformation—Germany—
Biography.   I. Title.
    BR325.R625 2010
    284.1092—dc22
    [B]
                                                                    2009033036

10 9 8 7 6 5 4 3 2 1

Longman
is an imprint of

www.pearsonhighered.com

ISBN-13: 978-0-205-60492-0
ISBN-10:   0-205-60492-7

Contents

Editor's Preface

"Biography is history seen through the prism of a person."

LOUIS FISCHER

It is often challenging to identify the roles and experiences of individuals in world history. Larger forces predominate. Yet biography provides important access to world history. It shows how individuals helped shape the society around them. Biography also offers concrete illustrations of larger patterns in political and intellectual life, in family life, and in the economy.

The Longman Library of World Biography series seeks to capture the individuality and drama that mark human character. It deals with individuals operating in one of the main periods of world history, while also reflecting issues in the particular society around them. Here, the individual illustrates larger themes of time and place. The interplay between the personal and general is always the key to using biography in history, and world history is no exception. Always, too, there is the question of personal agency: how much do individuals, even great ones, shape their own lives and environment, and how much are they shaped by the world around them?

PETER N. STEARNS

Author's Preface

More books have been written about Martin Luther than about anyone other than Jesus—a bit of information that can be found in several of the many available Luther biographies. So this book about the German reformer travels a well-trodden path. What distinguishes this biography from others is its intended audience. This is a book for people, especially students, who wish to understand Martin Luther within the broader sweep of history. Luther was a theologian, and theological issues are crucial for understanding him. But the larger context of Luther's life and its historical significance will also figure prominently in this account of his development, career, and thought. Occasional pauses in the narrative flow allow time for a fuller explanation of specific elements of the politics, society, and religion of Luther's day. In addition, sections titled "Writing History" introduce debates among historians about specific issues or events related to Luther's life.

This presentation divides Luther's life into four major themes, corresponding to the different vocations he had (some of them simultaneously): monk, professor, reformer, and preacher. Like most such schemes, it breaks down occasionally. The correspondence between these themes and the events of Luther's life is not always exact—for example, he was a preacher not only in the last decades of his life but for most of his career. The point is to provide an overarching idea and image to associate with a portion of Luther's life. The portraits of Luther in this volume have been chosen to enhance these themes. The title is a play on words that draws the themes together. Luther's was a life reformed in the usual sense of *reform*, that is, an improvement of its condition. In his case the reform was religious and profoundly affected his faith. The reform Luther preached to others had its origin in his own life. Luther's was also a life *re-formed* in the sense of being reshaped. The image he presented to the world reflected and promoted his activity, and he consciously appealed to his vocations as monk, professor, reformer, and preacher at crucial moments.

Selecting material for a biography of Martin Luther is a challenging and daunting task. In addition to the numerous volumes written about his life and times, Luther's own copious works fill over one hundred volumes in the standard critical edition. When confronted with a choice of appropriate material, I have chosen to quote those texts and narrate those events that provide the clearest insight into Luther's character or provide a window on the culture of his day. As a result, the biography often presents people and events as Luther viewed them. I have pointed out those times when Luther's view conflicts with more objective accounts. The reader should also bear in mind that this book is not a history of the Reformation. Other people and events related to the Reformation are introduced when they intersect with Luther's life, which does not necessarily reflect their importance for the course of the Reformation.

Luther wrote that history requires someone with "a lion's heart, unafraid to write the truth." He chided those historians who "readily pass over or put the best construction on the vices and deficiencies of their own times." I have tried to follow Luther's advice and not pass over his vices and deficiencies. This biography does not omit those writings and events that brought criticism upon Luther, both from his contemporaries and from subsequent generations of theologians and scholars. That is not to say that this book contains every bizarre or controversial thing Luther ever said. To do that would not only require a second volume this size, but it would also run the risk of rendering Luther's portrait in false tones. He lived in a day and age far removed from ours, and much that he said had a very different ring in the sixteenth century than it has today. Simply put, I have attempted to be even handed. Nevertheless, I suspect that some bias will show through. I am a Lutheran and, although I admire many of those who remained on the Catholic side of the divide, my sympathies ultimately lie with the Protestant Reformation.

My debts to other scholars are, of course, numerous. A small sense of what I owe to their works can be seen in the Note on the Sources. I would like to acknowledge my colleagues at Concordia Seminary for their help and encouragement, especially Professor Robert Kolb, who offered valuable comments on the manuscript at every stage. The encouragement and expertise of the Pearson editorial staff are also greatly appreciated, as are the comments of those who reviewed the manuscript: Patricia Ali, Morris College; Heather Bailey, University of Illinois at Springfield; Jean K. Berger, University of Wisconsin–Fox Valley; James W. Brodman, University of Central Arkansas; Gayle K. Brunelle, California State University–Fullerton; Francis A. Dutra, University of California–Santa Barbara; Martin Menke, Rivier College; Steven Ozment, Harvard University; Nathan B. Rein, Ursinus College; Jonathan Zophy, University of Houston–Clear Lake. Any errors that remain are entirely my own.

PAUL W. ROBINSON

Martin Luther

1

The Monk (1483–1511)

Introduction

"Help me, St. Anne! I will become a monk!" Martin Luther cried out as lightning struck perilously close. Caught in the open during a storm while he was walking back to the University of Erfurt, Martin feared for his life. That he should have called out to a saint for help required no explanation. Looking to the saints for deliverance in distress was as normal as breathing for men and women of that time. That Martin should have promised in that instant to trade his study of law for a life of religion, however, surprised even those who knew him best. In a flash, quite literally, Martin changed the course of his life, vowing to trade his master's robe for a monk's cowl. He would leave his friends and family to enter a monastery and, in so doing, embark on the journey that would make him the great reformer of European Christendom.

Early Life

Martin Luther was the second son of Hans and Margareta Luther. Although later in life Martin spoke of having come from peasant stock, his parents were upwardly mobile. Martin's mother, Margareta, came from a family that was well connected and by no means poor. That does not mean, however, that the Luthers were always well-to-do. In Saxony, where the Luther family lived, the law dictated that the youngest son inherit all of the father's property. Since Hans Luther was not the youngest son of his father, he could either work for his brother or strike out on his own. Hans chose to move his family to Mansfeld to work in the copper mines. Mining was a dirty and dangerous business, and Hans was determined not to remain a simple miner. In short order, he went into business for himself as a copper smelter, purifying the ore that the miners brought to the surface. He and his partners eventually ran several smelters, and Hans became financially comfortable if not wealthy. Comfort, however, came after Martin's childhood. His recollections of growing up portray a strict household with few resources. He told the story of how his mother had beaten his hands until they bled because he took a nut without permission.

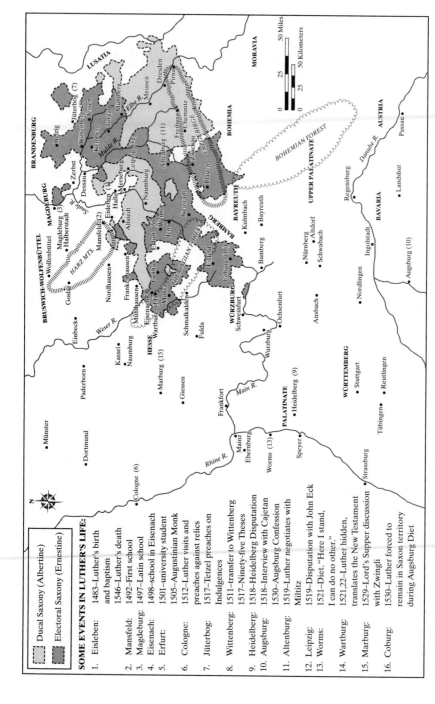

Map 1.1 Important places associated with Luther's life.

SOME EVENTS IN LUTHER'S LIFE:

1. Eisleben: 1483–Luther's birth and baptism
   1546–Luther's death
2. Mansfeld: 1492–First school
3. Magdeburg: 1497–Latin school
4. Eisenach: 1498–school in Eisenach
5. Erfurt: 1501–university student
   1505–Augustinian Monk
6. Cologne: 1512–Luther visits and preaches against relics
7. Jüterbog: 1517–Tetzel preaches on Indulgences
8. Wittenberg: 1511–transfer to Wittenberg
   1517–Ninety-five Theses
9. Heidelberg: 1518–Heidelberg Disputation
10. Augsburg: 1518–Interview with Cajetan
    1530–Augsburg Confession
11. Altenburg: 1519–Luther negotiates with Miltitz
12. Leipzig: 1519–Disputation with John Eck
13. Worms: 1521–Diet. "Here I stand, I can do no other."
14. Wartburg: 1521,22–Luther hidden, translates the New Testament
15. Marburg: 1529–Lord's Supper discussion with Zwingli
16. Coburg: 1530–Luther forced to remain in Saxon territory during Augsburg Diet

In its own small way the Luther household participated in sweeping changes to the European economy. The law that kept Hans from inheriting any part of the family farm also increased agricultural production by keeping larger plots of land together and causing them to be farmed more efficiently. The European population, growing once again after its devastation by plague in the fourteenth century, was on the move from the countryside to the towns and cities. Although this movement was nothing like the urbanization that would accompany the industrial revolution, people like Hans Luther demonstrated that European society was no longer defined primarily as those tied to the land governed by a small ruling class. Social mobility came with geographic mobility. People who made their way to the towns and cities also made a living there as artisans, craftsmen, or small business owners, contributing to economic growth and also raising their status in society. Even those bound to the land, if they could escape to the city and live there for a year and a day, would be declared free.

New endeavors marked this increasingly confident society. Christopher Columbus set sail from Spain when Martin Luther was eight years old. Throughout Europe merchants benefited from an increasing demand for luxury goods. The mining industry, more directly significant for our story, saw rapid technical advances. Gold, silver, and copper increased in value to the point that those who invested in better mining techniques could recoup their investment many times over. Hans Luther took advantage of this favorable climate in the mining business and, along with his partners, invested in the processing of copper ore. Being an independent businessman did not, however, guarantee that Hans enjoyed economic security. Those who rented the smelting rights from princes depended on their favor and were always in danger of losing their operation. Hans would never spend his hard-earned money freely.

In spite of the need for frugality, Hans Luther decided to invest in Martin's education. He could not have made that decision without careful thought. Only a very few people at the time received a formal education, and most of them were destined for careers in the church. Martin must have been an extremely intelligent boy for his family to decide that he should attend school. The only reason to go to school was to learn to read and speak Latin, and the only reason for learning Latin was to enter a university. So from the very beginning Hans meant to give his son a chance at a university education. Martin, for all his intelligence, was not an outstanding student in Latin school. Like the other students, he often failed to memorize his lessons correctly, and the teacher beat him like the others for his failure. Martin remembered his early school years with little fondness. Instead, he complained bitterly about the lack of imagination his teachers had shown in presenting their lessons, and he was convinced that beatings had not aided his learning in the slightest. Yet the Luther family had tried to obtain the best education possible for Martin; they sent him as a boarding student first to Magdeburg and then to Eisenach for a better education than he could receive in Mansfeld.

At Eisenach Martin found a teacher who inspired him and a home away from home. Although Martin had relatives in town, he was eventually taken into the home of Heinrich Schalbe, a leading citizen of Eisenach who even served a year-long term as mayor while Martin was in the city. The Schalbes became Martin's foster family, and later in life he referred to Frau Schalbe, his "landlady," with fondness. The religious life of Eisenach found profound expression in the Schalbe home. Heinrich patronized the Franciscan monastery, and a group of the monastery's supporters met regularly in his house. Martin later considered inviting this group to the celebration of his first Mass but did not, perhaps because he had become an Augustinian rather than a Franciscan! He clearly had a first-hand grasp of the monastic life as a result of his time with the Schalbes. Martin attended St. George's parish school in Eisenach. He said later that the teacher there was the best he had encountered. Martin also became part of an intellectual circle gathered by a learned priest in Eisenach, and through this group he first encountered the new worship service honoring St. Anne. Thus in Eisenach Martin's scholarly traits developed, along with his acquaintance with religious life, through the Franciscans and St. Anne—the saint to whom he would cry out in the thunderstorm a few years later.

The University of Erfurt

From grammar school in Eisenach Martin Luther went on to the university. He enrolled in the University of Erfurt in summer 1501. He was listed in the matriculation book as "Martin Luther from Mansfeld" and as a student who was able to pay something for his education rather than as a charity case. Erfurt was by far the largest city Martin had ever seen, and with its 20,000 inhabitants was one of the largest German cities. The university had not been founded by a prince but had arisen from the city schools and benefited from the number of students that came to it from the religious orders. The Augustinians, Franciscans, and Dominicans all had houses of studies in Erfurt, and from those schools, advanced students would go on to study theology at the University. Most universities in Europe, whether or not they were founded directly by the church, offered theological studies.

Medieval universities all followed the same pattern. Students began their studies in the arts faculties with Aristotelian philosophy aimed toward logical reasoning and argument. Only after obtaining a master of arts degree would students advance toward higher levels of study in the other faculties. Law, medicine, and theology were the three options for advanced study at this time. Although some universities specialized in just one of these subjects, most attempted to cover all three. Students who attended lectures did not necessarily stay at a university long enough to obtain even the master's degree, so the numbers in the higher faculties were always relatively small. The educational method employed by the higher faculties was similar regardless of the discipline. All instruction consisted of lectures and debates covering an authoritative text. There was little or no recourse to knowledge received by experience or experiment. So even in the medical faculties at this time, understanding was gained through a logical approach to textbooks. The standard approach to Aristotelian logic taught in the arts faculties served whether the student advanced to medicine, law, or theology.

Martin's living conditions at Erfurt were spartan. The routine of all students mimicked the monastery more than anything else. The students, all male in those days, lived together in common rooms, took their meals together, listened to lectures, studied, and attended worship services at the same time. Although many students spent their spare time drinking and fighting, Martin seems to have been a serious scholar who impressed his classmates with his intellect. Not all learning took place in the university classrooms. Renaissance humanism had made inroads in Erfurt, and several of Luther's classmates would become famous names among the German humanists. Humanism emphasized what many scholars had seen to be missing from the university curriculum. Instead of focusing primarily on Aristotle and logic, humanist teachers used all the Greek and Latin classical literature for its rhetorical and stylistic impact, its practical wisdom, and its historical and moral lessons. The humanists read these texts without the commentary of the medieval scholars, in contrast to the university approach that always used authoritative commentary to approach a text. Like-minded humanist teachers and students gathered in Erfurt, as in other cities, and pursued their own course of studies above and beyond that mandated by the university. Although how fully Martin participated in these studies is a matter of debate, he certainly encountered humanist ideas in Erfurt, and the humanist method of approaching a text became key to his later understanding of the Bible.

Martin's study bore fruit in January 1505 when he received the master of arts degree. He was mightily impressed by the ceremony, in which the graduates received lighted candles, and commented later that no earthly joy was greater than that moment. As a master, Martin would have begun to teach in the arts faculty of the university and was eligible to begin his studies in the higher faculty of law. He began his law studies in May, using the brand-new textbook his father had given him. This book, the *Corpus Iuris Civilis*, that is, the emperor Justinian's compilation of Roman Law, formed the basis of lectures in the law faculty. The book was an expensive present and a token of the investment that Hans Luther had made in his talented son. Yet only two months later Martin would make his vow to leave law school and become a monk. We can comprehend his thinking only through an understanding of the religious aspects of his upbringing and education.

Conversion to Monasticism

Martin had been taught to value spiritual security even more highly than economic security. Concern for the afterlife dominated church teaching. The faithful were to spend their life on earth preparing for the day when God would judge them according to their works. Many people lived in fear of being condemned to the eternal torment of hell on that day, and revival preachers heightened that fear with their vivid portrayals of the suffering of the damned in never-ending fires under the torment of innumerable demons. Those listening to the preachers also assumed that only saints, that is, people who were almost completely holy, would be welcomed immediately into the eternal joy of heaven. Those who were not bad enough for hell but not yet holy enough for heaven expected to spend a long time, usually thousands of years, in purgatory. The church offered the solution of its sacraments to the problem of one's eternal destiny. Through the seven

AETHERNA IPSE SVAE MENTIS SIMVLACHRA LVTHERVS
EXPRIMIT·AT VVLTVS CERA LV·CAE OCCIDVOS·

·M·D·XX·

Photo 1.1   Luther in a 1520 engraving by Lucas Cranach. He is tonsured and wears the Augustinian habit. Source: Art Resource, N.Y.

sacraments—baptism, penance, the Mass, confirmation, marriage, ordination, and last rites—the church delivered God's grace, that is, his power to forgive sins and do good works. Penance and the Mass, because they were the only sacraments that could be received more than once, were at the center of religious life. In 1215 church leaders had decreed at the Fourth Lateran Council that at least once a year every adult Christian had to receive communion, that is, take the body and blood of Christ under the form of bread and wine in the Mass, and receive the priest's forgiveness in penance before taking communion. The Mass also offered grace apart from receiving communion. Simply by being present when the priest said Mass, which was considered to be a sacrifice offered to God, the Christian received grace necessary to do good works.

In addition to these sacraments, the saints were considered powerful allies in the Christian life. All Christians in the late Middle Ages believed that holy men and women who had died, the saints, could intercede with God from their place in heaven on behalf of those who prayed to them. The intercession of the saints was part of the Mass, and the rood screen (so-called in English because it featured a cross, or rood) that separated the priest from the congregation during Mass was decorated with pictures of specific saints. Side altars in large churches were dedicated to saints. People also sought the help of the saints outside the church. A dizzying variety of specific problems and ailments each had a saint assigned for special care and help. Mary, the mother of Jesus, was the saint par excellence, and devotion to Mary played a crucial role in medieval religious life. Saying the rosary—the word referred to both a series of prayers to say and the beads that helped the faithful to count the prayers—had become popular in the fifteenth century. Among the prayers of the rosary were prayers directed to Mary. When Martin Luther prayed in the storm, he invoked St. Anne. St. Anne was also a powerful saint, being revered as the mother of Mary, and she was the patron saint of miners, so Martin would have been familiar with devotion to her. The power of the saints could also be accessed through relics—bones, or bits of bone, or pieces of clothing said to be from the saint. Relics were an important part of late medieval religious life. The most important relics became the object of religious travel, the pilgrimage. Relic collections provided places for devotion and, if the right prayers were said, offered relief from time to be spent in purgatory. As we will see, such a relic collection played an important part in Luther's composition of his *95 Theses*.

Martin's family participated fully and faithfully in this religious life. Hans and Margareta's son was named Martin because he was baptized on St. Martin's day, the day after his birth on November 10, 1483. That baptism brought him into the fold of the church and into the community; in the fifteenth century even citizens who were less than faithful Christians had been baptized and were formally members of the church. Hans Luther had every reason to be a pious man, if for no other reason than out of concern for his soul amidst the dangers to the body posed by the mining business. For precisely this reason, miners were devoted to St. Anne, the mother of Mary, as their special intercessor. Margareta, by all accounts, diligently taught her children what the church expected of them. Martin's own piety and his conversion to monasticism testify to a spiritual upbringing.

On July 2, 1505 Martin was on his way back to the university in Erfurt from Mansfeld, where his parents lived. We do not know why Martin had gone home, but there must have been good reason to make such a journey. Some think that he went to discuss with his father misgivings about becoming a lawyer. Others suggest that Hans had asked his son to come home in order to discuss marriage. Either matter would become irrelevant in the midst of the thunderstorm that suddenly came upon the traveler. When lightning struck nearby, Martin feared for his life. The terror over his eternal destiny engulfed him, and in a final effort to save himself he cried out to St. Anne. "Help me, St. Anne! I will become a monk!" he shouted. When Martin survived the storm, the matter, as far as he was concerned, was decided.

Martin's feelings of intense fear concerning God's judgment probably began before the vow to become a monk. Such feelings, though not the norm even for the late Middle Ages, were common enough that theologians had addressed them as a specific spiritual malady. For a person laboring under this kind of fear, the idea of becoming a monk or nun would have seemed an ideal solution. Most people thought the monastery provided a refuge from such spiritual despair. So when Martin vowed, in the midst of the storm, to become a monk, he had probably been mulling the idea over for some time. The lightning storm and the fear of sudden, violent death forced him to shout out a final answer to the question of his vocation.

Hans Luther was furious about his son's vow and, in the heat of the moment, disowned Martin. Only some weeks later did Hans reluctantly consent to his son's decision. Yet if Martin's family and friends were surprised by his decision, it could not have been entirely unexpected. A studious young man who was intensely concerned about his spiritual life made the ideal candidate for the monastery. As the first step to fulfilling the vow, Martin held a going-away party, distributed his worldly goods among his friends, and set off for the monastery of the Augustinian Hermits in Erfurt, the city where he had been attending university. Fifteen days after his vow in the storm, he appeared at the monastery gate and, as was the custom, asked to be admitted. Martin Luther would become a monk.

The Erfurt Augustinians

Martin Luther never explained why he chose the Augustinians over the many other orders that had monastic houses in Erfurt. He may have chosen them for their proximity to his student house, their reputation for rigorous observance of their monastic rule, their formal connection to the university, or their study of the works of their namesake, St. Augustine.

Augustinians were technically not monks but friars, meaning that they had originally begged for food and other necessities. By the time Martin joined the order, however, they had monasteries and churches along with steady streams of income. The practice of begging continued at Erfurt but as a ritual collection of support from the different regions of the city.

The structure of life in the monastery focused the monk's efforts on the highest level of Christian living. For the late Middle Ages that meant a daily round of prayer and good works, as well as the sacraments of penance and the Mass.

The earliest Christian monks were solitary figures—holy men who lived and prayed alone in the Egyptian desert. But the form of monasticism that took hold in the Christian West was communal. Monks lived and prayed together, and the earliest monastic rules for this communal life focused on a daily round of prayer services, the daily offices. In Luther's time the Augustinians in the Erfurt cloister prayed together seven times a day, as monks had for centuries. They began around 3 o'clock in the morning with Matins and concluded with Compline just before retiring at sunset. Such prayer was so much at the center of monastic life that those who missed the communal service, even for good reason, were expected to make up those prayers on their own. Luther once reported that he was several months behind in his prayers as a result of his teaching duties. Although prayer was the principle good work of the monks, they filled the time around their prayers with many other activities. The work of the Erfurt Augustinians embraced performing other duties in the cloister, studying and teaching at the University, and preaching and providing pastoral care in the city. In all of these activities the monk strove for attitudes and actions that most exemplified Christian virtues. Their life was a struggle for holiness.

Monks believed the sacraments of penance and the Mass could preserve them on their way to holiness. Remember that sacraments, according to medieval theologians, conveyed God's grace—the power to do good works—to those who received them. Taking monastic vows was in itself a sacrament. But once the monk had promised to obey the rule, he needed the sacrament of penance to make up for his failures. Penance consisted of confessing one's faults to a priest, usually another monk who had been ordained as a priest, and then receiving absolution, or forgiveness, along with a penance. The penance from which the sacrament took its name was an assignment, usually prayers or other good works, that would show that the one who confessed was truly sorry. Luther firmly embraced penance during his time in the monastery. He confessed frequently, reporting that on one occasion it took him six hours to confess all his faults. He performed his penance zealously, going far beyond what was actually required of him. In this way, he hoped for release from the crushing burden he felt because of his sins.

Monks, like all Christians at the time, looked to the Mass as the principle vehicle of God's grace. Mass was celebrated each day in the Erfurt cloister, publicly and also privately by every Augustinian who was also an ordained priest. Although in the Early Middle Ages few monks were also priests, that had changed by Luther's time. The increasing importance of the Mass as a sacrifice, as a good work that could be offered on behalf of others, meant that more and more monks became priests, too, so that they could perform this good work. The Erfurt Augustinians, like other monks, relied on the money they could earn by saying Mass for others. Unlike the laity, who participated by watching the Mass, the priest offered the sacrifice each day—lifting up the bread that, according to church teaching, was Christ's body and the chalice that contained Christ's blood. In this way the priest communicated with God directly. The sacrifice of the Mass was an awesome responsibility, and becoming a priest marked a turning point in Luther's monastic career.

A monk with Luther's level of education would naturally become a priest. Brother Martin prepared for his ordination, the church ceremony by which a man was made a priest, by studying books that discussed the theology and practice of the Mass. The books treated the matter thoroughly, always underscoring the role of the priest, that is, the priest's power to celebrate Mass, and emphasizing that in the Mass the priest needed to be holy because he handled bread and wine that miraculously became the body and blood of Christ. Following Martin's ordination, the monastery hosted a festive celebration of his first Mass on May 2, 1507. Martin was allowed to invite his family and friends for this celebration. Hans Luther came from Mansfeld with twenty others and paid the monastery a fairly large sum to put them up. Martin still remembered his father's contribution twenty-five years later even as he remembered his own moment of hesitation during the Mass.

> When at length I stood before the altar and was to consecrate, I was so terrified by the words *aeterno vivo vero Deo* [to you the eternal, living, true God] that I thought of running away from the altar and said to my prior, "Reverend Father, I'm afraid I must leave the altar." He shouted to me, "Go ahead, faster, faster!"

Martin firmly believed that as the priest celebrating Mass, he stood directly in the presence of God, and he believed just as firmly that he was entirely unworthy of that presence. Such beliefs would profoundly shape his life.

Anfechtungen and the Study of Theology

Martin's sense of despair over his inability to do enough good to please God haunted him. Although this feeling may have preceded his time as monk and driven him into the monastery in the first place, his doubts continued even as he exerted himself in prayer and penance as a monk. He referred to these attacks of doubt as *Anfechtungen*, and most scholars of Luther use this term without translating it. Simply put, Martin feared God's judgment, believing that he would be condemned to hell. Johann von Staupitz, the Augustinian official who became Martin's mentor, tried to convince the young monk that God was also merciful and was gracious to those who, like Martin, feared him. Luther later credited Staupitz with encouraging him to trust in Christ for salvation. But during his time in the monastery, Martin also feared Jesus Christ as his judge—and not without reason since Christ was often portrayed as judge of the world in medieval art.

Staupitz, in an apparent attempt to drive his message of God's grace home to Martin, sent him back to the university but this time to study theology. Martin devoted himself to study and greatly respected his teachers. But the theology they taught him did nothing to alleviate his feelings of guilt and fear before God. The nominalist school of theology dominated Erfurt at this time. Nominalism originated with William of Ockham, a fourteenth-century Franciscan and teacher at Oxford University, as a philosophical position centered on the idea that human knowledge is derived from an understanding of individual things rather than coming through preexisting, universal ideas.

Ockham also emphasized the power of God and God's concomitant freedom to act as he chose, and many of his followers applied these ideas broadly and thoroughly to theological issues. Nominalist theologians believed that God had chosen to save those who did their best to please him by good works. Good works were rewarded by God with grace through the church and its sacraments. This grace empowered people to do more good works and, through this cooperation between works and grace, to reach the point of being accepted by God and rewarded with eternal life in heaven when they died. Such ideas simply confirmed Martin in his despair over his own inability to produce works that he thought were truly good in God's sight.

Nevertheless, Martin continued with his studies, which also included teaching the Bible and Peter Lombard's *Sentences*, the main theological textbook of the Middle Ages. His study and teaching of Lombard's *Sentences* acquainted him with the answers medieval theologians had given to a vast array of questions. His study of the Bible led him to search for his own answers to the more personal questions that arose from his own feelings of guilt and despair. Martin might well have remained to study and teach at Erfurt for many years had it not been for a trip to Rome.

Journey to Rome

Luther entered the Augustinian order in the midst of dissension over how reform in the order should proceed. The Erfurt monastery participated in a wider movement of reform among the Saxon monasteries, meaning that they wished to observe their rule more rigorously than other Augustinian monasteries. Staupitz, Luther's superior and mentor, had succeeded in his plan to unite these reformed monasteries with a group of Augustinian monasteries in Lombardy (northern Italy). Through this union Staupitz wished to gain the papal privileges, especially freedom from the oversight of certain bishops and monastic officials, enjoyed by the Lombard monasteries. In this way he hoped to promote the reform movement. After negotiation with the minister general of the Augustinians, Staupitz gained permission for the union and made it public in 1510.

The Augustinian monks of Erfurt rebelled at the prospect of being united with the unreformed Lombard monasteries. The monks believed that they might be kept from their own strict observance in order to accommodate the others. So the monks sent two of their number, Johann Nathin and Martin Luther, to appeal the decision to the Archbishop of Magdeburg. When the archbishop denied the appeal, the monks resolved to appeal to the Augustinian minister general in Rome. So Martin Luther and another monk, whose name has been lost to us, set off for Rome.

Martin spoke of his journey to Rome and the time he spent there throughout his life. Although his scattered comments do not allow us to trace his route to and from Rome with any precision, his travels made an impression. He later remembered the generally good nature of the people he encountered, even though as he traveled into southern Germany he could no longer understand the dialects being spoken. He said little about the large cities but much about the farmland, noting that the grapes and peaches were both much larger in Italy than in Germany. The Italian people did not fare as well in Luther's assessment as their produce. Although the Italians did not drink as much as the Germans, Martin also thought they were much less pious. He recalled the richness of some of the abbeys in which he was a guest, perhaps implicitly criticizing their lifestyle compared to that of the monks in his own observant monastery in Erfurt.

When Martin arrived in Rome, he saw a city fallen from its imperial grandeur. Ruins like the colosseum dominated the landscape, the old city walls encircled much land that was now barren or used for crops, and the papacy provided the city's only real business. That business, however, brought people to Rome as plaintiffs in lawsuits, as office-seekers, and as pilgrims. The papal courts did a brisk business hearing appeals from lower church courts. The palaces of the cardinals welcomed a steady stream of men looking for a lucrative position in the church. At times the streets thronged with pilgrims—religious tourists visiting shrines, hearing Mass, and buying souvenirs. While Martin was walking the streets, Michelangelo was at work on the ceiling of the Sistine chapel. The pope who commissioned this work, Julius II, had also recently begun to rebuild St. Peter's basilica. Later, Luther would write his famous 95 Theses in response to an indulgence whose proceeds would go to continue the work on this church.

While in Rome, Martin behaved as a typical pilgrim who was also a priest. He visited the churches and viewed the relics that made up the standard pilgrim's route in Rome. He wished to make a full confession of his sins but reported that he could not find a priest with sufficient knowledge to hear his confession. (It was the responsibility of the one making a confession to ensure that the priest hearing it was qualified.) He stood in long lines of priests to say Mass at the altars of Rome's churches. Martin recalled that, because he said Mass more slowly than the Italians, the priests in line behind him shouted at him to hurry up. He also went to the Lateran palace complex to climb the "Holy Stairs," 28 steps that Jesus himself supposedly ascended when he was being judged by the Roman governor Pontius Pilate. Martin climbed the stairs on his knees and prayed an Our Father on each step. He believed, as he had been told, that this action could release a soul from purgatory, and he dedicated his devotion to the soul of his deceased grandfather. In a sermon preached a year before his death, Luther recalled wondering at the time, "Who knows if it is true?"

Yet the result of Martin's visit to Rome was apparently not, as for many others at the time, a feeling of despair concerning the state of the church. He returned to the monastery in Erfurt much as he had left it—as a pious and faithful monk concerned for his own salvation. But the result of the official business that took him to Rome proved crucial for his future. The appeal of the Erfurt Augustinians was denied, and Martin proclaimed his obedience to Staupitz. Outrage from the other monks greeted this decision. In order to protect Martin from their persecution, Staupitz ordered him to Wittenberg, the capital of Electoral Saxony, to teach theology in the new University there. Martin Luther, Augustinian monk and student of theology, was to become a professor.

Writing History: Erikson's *Young Man Luther*

Historians who work to reconstruct the events of Luther's early life often stand on less-than-solid ground. Luther's own statements about his youth come from much later in his life and are often used to make a particular point rather than simply to give an account of his development. He himself was not even sure about the year of his birth. His first biographers were either friends intent on portraying him heroically or enemies intent on showing him to be a depraved heretic. So information gleaned from these early biographies stands in need of significant historical interpretation.

Yet greatness seems to require an explanation. In earlier times a remarkable human being might have been considered favored by fortune or the gods and his or her life attended by omens or prophecies. In our own day an explanation for greatness is sought in temperament or upbringing. For this reason scholars have exerted tremendous effort to document and understand Luther's early life. Some have focused on his education and the influential ideas of his day. Others have sought explanations in his career as a monk or his interaction with colleagues at the University of Wittenberg.

Erik Erikson, a Freudian psychoanalyst, crafted one of the more provocative interpretations of Luther's early life. His *Young Man Luther: A Study in Psychoanalysis and History* attempted to put Luther on the psychiatrist's couch some 400 years after his death. Erikson approaches Luther's life from the standpoint of identity formation, an area of psychiatry in which Erikson was a pioneer. For Erikson, Luther's conflict with his father—the Freudian Oedipal complex—is key. Luther formed his identity by searching for a father figure first in the monastery and finally in God, whom Luther first believed to be disapproving and condemning like his father, Hans. Thus the psychoanalyst sees Luther's breakthrough understanding (see the "Writing History" section in Chapter 2) as a resolution of this search for a father figure consisting in his discovery that God was indeed gracious and had forgiven him.

Numerous historians criticized Erikson's work. As they correctly observed, he had stepped outside the bounds of what historians are able to say based on the surviving evidence. All accounts of Luther's early life are based on scanty evidence, much of it his own reminiscences later in life. Moreover, specific incidents can be interpreted in different ways. For example, Luther recalled that his father once beat him and that it took them some time to reconcile. Erikson used this story to assume a pattern of behavior between father and son. Other interpreters assume that Luther told about the beating as something that stood out in his memory precisely because his father had not normally behaved in this way. These are the kinds of judgment calls that historians frequently make, and one could argue persuasively for either interpretation. At times, however, Erikson used information that is itself questionable. He relied heavily on a story told by Luther's enemies about how the young monk had once acted as if he were possessed by a demon. Although Erikson accepted the stories told by Luther's foes, he assumed that Luther himself had later stated as fact things that happened at the time only in his mind. For example, Erikson did not believe that the verbal exchange Luther recounted in connection with his first Mass (see the section titled "Erfurt Augustinians" in this chapter) actually took place. He believed that Luther merely thought at the time what he later related as being spoken. Despite the criticism, Erikson's interpretation influenced some historians toward a brief flourishing of psychohistory as a genre of historical writing.

Erikson correctly criticizes a tendency to make Luther—and, we might add, other significant individuals—more heroic than they really were. Historians study human beings about whom they can know only from what has remained in the sources. Because so many possibly important words and events remain unknown, historians can never speak the final word about why individuals thought or acted as they did but only suggest the most plausible reasons.

Luther in His Own Words: 1545 Preface to a Collection of Luther's Works in Latin (Selections)

The selections that follow are from a preface that Martin Luther wrote in 1545, a year before his death. The preface is autobiographical. In it, Luther explained the events that formed the background for his early writings. In the paragraphs presented here, he warns the reader that he no longer agrees with everything he wrote early in his career, describes his time as a monk in exaggerated terms, and recalls how through his lectures he reached his Reformation breakthrough—an event that we will consider in Chapter 2.

> But I ask before all else, pious reader, and I ask because of our Lord Jesus Christ, that you read those things [i.e., his earliest writings] judiciously, indeed with great compassion. And let the reader understand that when I began my work I was a monk and a most insane papist. I was so drunk, yes, drowned in the pope's teachings, that I was ready if I were able to kill, or to cooperate with and consent to killing, everyone who refused even one syllable of obedience to the pope. So great a Saul* was I!—as many still are. I was not cold and reserved in defending the papacy, as Eck† and his like were. They seemed to me to defend the pope not because they took the matter seriously but for their own material gain. To this very day it seems to me as if they, like Epicureans, are laughing at the pope. I took the matter seriously. I was terribly afraid of the Day of Judgment, and I longed in the depths of my being to be saved.
>
> Meanwhile in that year [1519] I returned a second time to the interpretation of the Psalms, confident that I was more experienced after I had expounded in the classroom the epistles of St. Paul to the Romans and Galatians and also the epistle to the Hebrews. I had been overcome by an astonishing passion for understanding Paul in the letter to the Romans. Until then it had not been a lack of desire that stopped me from understanding it but one little phrase in chapter one: the righteousness of God is revealed in that. How I hated the phrase

---

*Saul was the Apostle Paul's name before his conversion. Under the name Saul he had persecuted Christians.

righteousness of God. The example and practice of all the experts had taught me to understand it philosophically as if it meant, as they said, the formal or active justice by which God is just and by which he punishes the unjust and sinners.

But I, even though I was living as a blameless monk, felt I was a sinner with a disturbed conscience before God, and I could not believe firmly that my satisfaction was pleasing to God. I did not love—indeed I hated the just God who punishes sinners. I was indignant with God—I did not actually blaspheme because I kept silent but I murmured greatly—and I thought: As if it is not enough that miserable sinners and those eternally condemned by original sin[1] are oppressed by every kind of calamity through the law of the Ten Commandments, but God adds sorrow to sorrow through the gospel.[2] Even through the gospel God stretches out toward us with justice and wrath. So I was frantic with a furious and disturbed conscience. I, being insolent, was hammering away at Paul there [i.e., Romans 1:17 where the phrase *righteousness of God* occurs], most ardently thirsting to know what Saint Paul was trying to say.

Then by the mercy of God meditating day and night I paid attention to the context of the words: "The righteousness of God is revealed in it, just as it is written, 'The righteous one will live by faith.'" There I began to understand the righteousness of God through which the righteous person lives by the gift of God, to be sure, by faith. This is what it means: The righteousness of God is made known by the gospel. That righteousness of the gospel does not require a person to do anything. It is the righteousness by which the merciful God makes sinners righteous through faith, just as it is written: "The righteous one will live by faith." Here I felt that I had in a way been born again. I felt as if the gates of heaven had been opened and I had gone into paradise itself.

---

[1]The sins of the first people believed to have been inherited by all human beings since.
[2]Gospel means *good news*. Here Luther argues against an understanding of the biblical gospel that, to his mind, was not good news but only made people more fearful.

2

The Professor (1512–1519)

Introduction

"I reserve for myself this alone, which indeed must be reserved, that a council has erred at times and is able to err at any time, especially in those things that do not concern the faith. Nor does a council have authority to establish new articles of faith, otherwise we would have as many such articles as there are human opinions." With these words, spoken in an academic debate with Dr. Johann Eck in Leipzig, Martin Luther declared his freedom from medieval notions of church authority. The statement represents a radical break with tradition and an equally radical reliance on Scripture, the only authority that remained for him after rejecting popes and councils. How Martin Luther came to this point has everything to do with the position as university professor assigned to him in the wake of his journey to Rome.

Luther's role as professor of Bible at the University of Wittenberg helped to form the ideas and shape the events that thrust him into prominence and that would come to be seen as the beginning of the Protestant Reformation. In this chapter we will consider a period (1512–1519) that is dominated by the activities of a professor, especially lectures and academic disputations. Luther's lectures to his students helped him gradually to shape his ideas about salvation and led him to an understanding that was opposed to the dominant theology of the day. Three disputations, the first of which never got past the stage of theses for debate, made Luther a household name—a proposed disputation on indulgences, the Heidelberg disputation, and the Leipzig disputation. Along the way, Luther the professor gained some important colleagues in the work of reform and also earned some powerful opponents, including the pope himself.

Wittenberg

When Martin Luther returned from his 1510 trip to Rome, he acknowledged that Staupitz had the right to combine the two branches of the Augustinian order. In so doing, he placed himself in an adversarial position to his fellow monks in Erfurt, and this led Staupitz eventually to assign him to Wittenberg as the Bible lecturer at the university. Staupitz himself had assumed this position as a personal favor to Elector Frederick, the ruler of Electoral Saxony, but under the press of the order's business had been increasingly unable to fulfill his duties in Wittenberg. One day in the monastery courtyard, under the shade of a pear tree, Staupitz informed Brother Martin that he was to take his doctorate and begin teaching at the University of Wittenberg. Martin was reluctant to obey, protesting that he was not ready to assume such a responsibility. But Staupitz insisted on the change—as much to provide for his protégé a friendlier environment and a classroom outlet for his restless intellect as to free himself from the obligation.

Arriving in Wittenberg in 1511, Luther would have noticed that it was little more than a town when compared to a city like Erfurt. The elector had only recently made Wittenberg his capital as a result of a division of Saxony that had left Duke George, his cousin, in possession of the city of Leipzig with Saxony's only university. George ruled the better part of Saxony but Frederick had the title of elector, meaning that he was one of seven rulers who elected the Holy Roman Emperor. And Frederick was determined to make Wittenberg a capital worthy of his electoral dignity. He had already rebuilt the castle and its church when Luther arrived. More important for our story, in 1502 Frederick had founded the university that was to be the scene of Luther's activity. Luther's teaching would put the new university and the city of Wittenberg on the map in a way that Elector Frederick could not have imagined.

The University of Wittenberg awarded Martin Luther the doctor's degree in October 1512. As part of the ceremony Luther swore to teach nothing contrary to church teaching. He also received the symbols of his office, including a biretta (the cap he is often pictured wearing) and a golden doctor's ring. Elector Frederick paid the fees necessary for the ceremony out of his treasury. Although Luther had invited his fellow monks from Erfurt to attend, they boycotted the ceremony. The Erfurters believed that Luther should have taken the degree there since he had begun his advanced studies at the University of Erfurt. Luther countered that it was a misunderstanding and that since he had also studied in Wittenberg, he had every right to become a doctor there. Though the issue may seem unimportant, Luther regretted the rift between himself and the monks of Erfurt and was forced from the beginning to defend his new position.

Colleagues

In Wittenberg Luther also found a group of colleagues who would help him test and then promote his ideas in the years to come. Several members of the university faculty that Luther joined would play important roles in Luther's development and in the Reformation. Nikolaus von Amsdorf, a Wittenberg theologian and nephew of Staupitz, became one of Luther's first adherents and a close friend. Andreas Bodenstein von Karlstadt, another theologian, tended to push Luther's ideas to their ultimate conclusion and would emerge as a reformer in his own right, albeit more radical than Luther and ultimately in opposition to him.

Two remarkable individuals in the employ of Elector Frederick, Georg Spalatin and Lucas Cranach the Elder, would also provide crucial assistance to

Photo 2.1 This painting by Lucas Cranach shows Luther as he would have appeared in the classroom early in his career as professor at Wittenberg. Source: The Bridgeman Art Library International.

Luther. Spalatin was a humanist who studied at the universities of Erfurt and Wittenberg and eventually became a priest. He began his service to the elector by building his library collection but soon joined the electoral government. He served as Elector Frederick's private secretary and spiritual advisor, becoming the elector's principal counselor on church and university matters. In this role, he represented Luther to the elector and vice versa. During the crucial early years of the Reformation, Spalatin promoted Luther's cause at the Saxon court and, equally important, restrained Luther when he became impetuous. The number of letters exchanged between Luther and Spalatin peaked in 1521, a high point of Reformation activity. Indeed, whenever Luther's relations with the elector are narrated in this volume, it can be assumed that Spalatin served as the intermediary. As Luther's link to Elector Frederick, Spalatin provided the reformer with a window to the world of politics in Saxony and in the empire. Spalatin, for his part, became increasingly interested in biblical studies through his friendship with Professor Luther.

Lucas Cranach had served as artist to the Electoral Saxon Court since 1505. Born in 1473 in southern Germany, Cranach received his basic artistic education from his father. As a young man, he traveled as far as Vienna and spent several years there before his appointment by Elector Frederick as court artist. Cranach quickly established an artistic workshop in Wittenberg. In addition to providing decorative works for the elector's castles, Cranach and his assistants painted portraits of many prominent individuals, including Luther. The most well-known images of the reformer were etched or painted by Cranach. In paintings that still surround the altar of the city church in Wittenberg, Cranach depicted all the major Wittenberg reformers engaged in various church activities. (The picture of Luther preaching used in this volume comes from that group of paintings.) Cranach portrayed Luther's image for the rest of Europe and also presented Luther's ideas in an artistic fashion through the production of woodcut illustrations for printing. For example, Luther commissioned Cranach to produce woodcuts for the book of Revelation in his German translation of the Bible. As a citizen of Wittenberg, Cranach became prosperous and prominent. He eventually acquired an entire complex of buildings that housed his family and workshop as well as being hired out for other business interests, such as a printing press. Cranach also served two terms as mayor of the city.

The environment of Wittenberg, especially its university, and men like Amsdorf, Kalrstadt, Spalatin, and Cranach provided impetus and occasion, personnel, critique, and support for what would come to be called the Protestant Reformation. But that was all in the future when Luther entered the Wittenberg university classroom to offer his first lectures as a professor.

Lectures on the Bible

Luther's lectures on Psalms are the earliest that have been preserved for us. (He may or may not have lectured on another book of the Bible before Psalms.) The new professor spent the years from 1513 to 1515 explaining to his class these 150 biblical songs or poems. He prepared his lecture notes in advance—both brief comments on individual words or phrases and more extended commentary on the text. These notes were written on pages specially prepared for him by the local printer. Each page had a portion of the Psalms printed in the center with space between the lines and wide margins left blank for notes. The students—there were about 150 when Luther first arrived in Wittenberg—found their seats in the lecture hall early in the morning (6 A.M. in summer and 7 A.M. in winter). They would write as Luther dictated his notes to them until lunchtime.

Luther probably gravitated to the Psalms as a lecture topic because, as a monk, he had been reciting every one of the Psalms once a week over the previous eight years and as a result knew them well. In these lectures Luther shows himself to be a scholar steeped in the medieval method of understanding Scripture. That method started with the assumption that behind the obvious, literal sense of the language of the biblical books stood a deeper and more meaningful spiritual or allegorical sense. This idea helped medieval scholars to explain how parts of the Bible that appeared mundane or even profane could nevertheless be meant to communicate something about God. By day Bible scholars had settled on four primary senses of the biblical text—the literal (the plain sense of the words), the allegorical (a meaning in reference to Christ or the church), the tropological (a meaning in reference to moral behavior), and the anagogical (a meaning in reference to the afterlife or the end of the world). So, for example, Luther explained to his students in his lecture on Psalm 42, "Jordan is the river flowing through the midst of the Holy Land, but mystically it denotes Baptism in the church and Holy Scripture, in which all Christians are bathed." In this case, Luther uses the allegorical sense of the text, connecting the water of the Jordan with the water of baptism and the idea of Scripture as a spring of water, and shows how scholars in his time were able to discover references to Christ and the Christian church even in Old Testament books.

But the Psalms lectures also reveal that Luther continued to struggle with his own sense of despair and that he delved into Scripture in order to find an answer to it. He began to express the idea that to be a righteous person did not mean living without sin but instead meant recognizing sin and being willing to judge oneself. "For the righteous man is, first of all, one who is the accuser and condemner and judge of himself." God recognized as righteous, or justified, those who recognized sin in themselves and had faith in God. Luther put it this way in his lecture:

> For we are still unrighteous and unworthy before God, so that whatever we can do is nothing before Him. Yes, even faith and grace, through which we are today justified, would not of themselves justify us if God's covenant did not do it. It is precisely for this reason that we are saved: He made a testament and covenant with us that whoever believes and is baptized shall be saved.

We hear in these words echoes of Luther's own struggle. He expounded the psalms in a way that was not merely academic, though scholastic minutiae abound in the lectures, but personal and spiritual. In this, he followed the monastic and mystical tradition of discovering a profoundly personal application of the biblical text.

Yet Luther moved beyond the monastic and mystical approach in doggedly pursuing an understanding of righteousness beyond the good works prescribed by the church. Luther's decision to lecture on St. Paul's letter to the Romans after lecturing on Psalms gives a clear indication of the questions he was trying to answer. When he entered the lecture hall in spring 1515, he began, or perhaps continued, his struggle to understand what St. Paul had to say about salvation. Luther later remembered his insight into what Paul meant by the righteousness of God as a moment of breakthrough—the moment commonly referred to as Luther's "gospel discovery." Although historians continue to debate about precisely when that breakthrough took place and precisely what it is (see "Writing History" section in this chapter), we can find the principal element in Luther's lecture on Romans 1:17.

In human teachings the righteousness of man is revealed and taught, that is, who is and becomes righteous before himself and before other people and how this takes place. Only in the Gospel is the righteousness of God revealed (that is, who is and becomes righteous before God and how this takes place) by faith alone, by which the Word of God is believed, as it is written in the last chapter of Mark: "He who believes and is baptized will be saved; but he who does not believe will be condemned." For the righteousness of God is the cause of salvation. And here again, by the righteousness of God we must not understand the righteousness by which He is righteous in Himself but the righteousness by which we are made righteous by God. This happens through faith in the Gospel.

Whether or not this analysis struck Luther himself or his students as a breakthrough at the time, it became the foundation for his break with medieval tradition.

Luther's understanding of the relationship between righteousness and faith, taken to its logical conclusion, overturned much of scholastic theology, and especially the explanation theologians had given about how God saved people. All the medieval theologians agreed that good works, that is, human righteousness, played some role in salvation. The nominalists, representatives of the dominant theological approach in Luther's time, went so far as to say the human beings could produce good works without God's help and God would reward those good works with the grace that would aid people on the path toward salvation. Even those who did not go as far as the nominalists believed that human righteousness was the necessary goal of the Christian life. Such ideas received support from Aristotle's concept of *habit*, meaning acquiring a trait or characteristic through constant practice. Medieval theologians applied the idea of *habit* to righteousness— if you wish to be righteous, try to do righteous things. Luther, working with his new understanding of Romans, came to believe that righteousness from God, rather than the practice of human righteousness, was the foundation of the Christian life. This righteousness became for Luther the beginning—not the goal— of the Christian life. Good works resulted from this righteousness. So in contrast to the medieval theologians, Luther believed that Christians first became righteous and then were able to do righteous things.

In the years 1518 and 1519 Luther began to distinguish clearly between righteousness from God given to people through faith, and human righteousness. For example, in a 1519 sermon titled *Two Kinds of Righteousness*, Luther described the righteousness from God the Father as the righteousness of Jesus Christ, God's Son, given to human beings. "Through faith in Christ, therefore, Christ's righteousness becomes our righteousness and all that he has becomes ours. . . . This righteousness is primary; it is the basis, the cause, the source of all our own actual righteousness." Human righteousness was not a *requirement* for salvation but the *result* of being saved. God gave the righteousness needed for salvation to everyone who had faith, that is, trusted in Christ as the fulfillment of God's promise to save.

After Professor Luther concluded the Romans lectures in 1516, he turned his attention from Romans to Paul's letter to the Galatians and then to the book of Hebrews. More and more in these lectures he turned away from the medieval method of finding multiple meanings in the text. Instead, he used the original languages of the text—Hebrew for the Old Testament and Greek for the New Testament. Luther was able to do this because humanist scholars had worked to make tools and texts available, especially for the study of Greek. In 1516 Desiderius Erasmus, the great northern European humanist and scholar of the Greek language, published his edition of the Greek New Testament. This publication is a specific example of a general interest in better texts of the literature of the classical world among humanists. Humanists were interested not only in better texts but also in better understanding of those texts. They studied the history of the classical world in order to discover what the ancient texts had originally meant. As a result, humanists broke with the medieval method that was more interested in the comments of other scholars on the text than with what they might have meant originally. Luther relied on humanist method and humanist editions of texts in his biblical work. Had Luther stopped there, he might have remained a competent but relatively unknown scholar. He also began, however, to apply the theological insights he gained to his duties as a pastor, and that application led in short order to the indulgence controversy.

The Indulgence Controversy

When Martin Luther posted his *95 Theses* on the door of the castle church in Wittenberg, he was exercising his rights and, in his own mind at least, fulfilling his responsibilities as a professor of theology. Professors sought the truth in disputed or questionable matters, most often through debating each other. Theses—statements that could be defended or rejected in the argument—provided the structure for debates. Debaters would present arguments from logic or authorities, such as the Bible or the church fathers, in support of or against the theses. Very often such debates were held in conjunction with university studies, either when a student received a degree or as part of routine practice to sharpen logical and rhetorical skills. Debates might also be held for a specific purpose, and the *95 Theses* can be seen as an attempt to begin this kind of debate. In the preface to his theses Luther invited those who could not be present for the debate to submit their opinions in writing, suggesting that copies could be distributed outside of Wittenberg to foster theological conversation.

Yet Luther clearly meant his *95 Theses* to serve as more than a catalyst for casual debate. Luther's thinking about the practice of indulgences did not begin with but culminated in the theses. His ideas about indulgences were not evolving but had been formed, and he had anticipated the criticisms that would come from advocates of the indulgence trade. What he had failed to anticipate was the turmoil those ideas would cause and the financial interest highly placed church leaders had in the effective pursuit of indulgence sales. Archbishop Albrecht of Mainz, who had authorized and would profit from the indulgence sale in Germany, received from Luther a copy of the theses along with what is in retrospect a naïve cover letter. Luther initially failed to understand what was at stake politically in his theological opposition to indulgences. So to understand the controversy, we must explore both the general practice of indulgence sales and the specific politics behind the 1517 indulgence sale in Germany.

The *95 Theses* strike the modern reader as arcane rather than revolutionary because most of them concerned fine points of the medieval theology of indulgences. The idea of an indulgence itself requires explanation in order to understand Luther's theses. The indulgence arose from the practice of the sacrament of penance. In penance the Christian man or woman confessed his or her sins to the priest and expressed sorrow for those sins. The priest then pronounced absolution, that is, declared those sins forgiven, and assigned a penance. The penance was a task that confirmed the sincerity of the person's sorrow over the sins committed and expressed the desire to live a better life. Very often the penance consisted of a certain number of prayers to be said, although in earlier times it had been righting the wrong that had been committed. For example, if someone had stolen from a neighbor, the penance consisted of returning the stolen goods.

Originally an indulgence had simply meant that the person who had been assigned a specific penance was allowed to substitute some other good work instead. During the crusades, crusaders came to be recruited with the offer of a plenary indulgence. A plenary indulgence remitted all penances that had been assigned to someone but not completed, up to the time the indulgence was acquired. Because penance had grown in importance in the life of the church and because the amount of penance assigned had increased, most people had been assigned more penances than they could realistically accomplish. For this reason, a plenary indulgence was attractive and seemed an appropriate compensation for those willing to risk their lives fighting in the Holy Land. Those who contributed money to a crusader but did not go on crusade themselves were eventually allowed to receive the plenary indulgence as well. Soon the indulgences were available for a cash payment. The plenary indulgence received a wider circulation in 1300, which the pope declared a year of special celebration called a jubilee year. As part of the celebration, the pope offered plenary indulgences for sale more widely than ever before, and his successors continued that practice.

So by Luther's time *indulgence* had come to mean a piece of paper that promised remission of all penances (assuming that the person had confessed to a priest) and that was offered for purchase according to a sliding price scale depending on the buyer's station in society. Moreover, people commonly believed that the indulgence did more than remove penance—they believed that it guaranteed forgiveness for even the most heinous sins. Luther vehemently opposed such beliefs in his theses. But he also addressed more worldly financial concerns, since such concerns were at the heart of this particular sale of indulgences.

Half of the profit from the indulgence sale that prompted Luther's 95 *Theses* repaid a loan that was taken out by the Archbishop of Mainz from a banker in Augsburg to pay the pope in Rome. The diocese of Mainz elected Albrecht von Hohenzollern archbishop in 1514. The election represented a triumph for the Hohenzollern family since Albrecht as Archbishop of Mainz would join his brother, Joachim of Brandenburg, as one of seven electors of the Holy Roman Empire. In order to occupy this coveted position, Albrecht had only to pay the necessary fees to the pope. These included a fee for becoming archbishop, a portion of the first year's income of the diocese, and a fee for a dispensation for pluralism. (Albrecht was already bishop of Magdeburg and, according to church law should not have been able to take another position. Pluralism of this sort, however, had become common in the Middle Ages, and the popes, for a fee, routinely granted dispensations that excused officeholders from this point of canon law.) The total came to 29,000 gulden, a sum of money that far exceeded Albrecht's or his family's resources. As a point of comparison, Lucas Cranch received the substantial income of 100 gulden annually for his services as artist to the Saxon elector.

Jakob Fugger, head of a mercantile and banking empire centered in Augsburg, struck a deal with the pope that solved Albrecht's financial problem. Jakob Fugger loaned money to Albrecht to pay the fee. In return, Albrecht would lead a sale of indulgences in Germany. The pope encouraged such sales in order to raise money to build St. Peter's, the new papal church in Rome. Half of the proceeds from Albrecht's sale, however, would go to the Augsburg bank to repay the loan. So Albrecht became archbishop, the bank received a tidy return on its loan, and the pope gained a very motivated promulgator of indulgence sales in Germany. Albrecht chose John Tetzel, a Dominican, to head up the indulgence sale. Tetzel and others engaged by him would travel through Germany preaching to encourage the people to buy indulgences. In his own preaching and in his instructions to others concerning the indulgence, Tetzel highly praised the indulgence. He claimed, for example, that "whoever has an indulgence has salvation; anything else is of no avail." Wherever the indulgence preachers traveled, their message was reinforced by a large cross that displayed the papal bull authorizing the indulgence along with a money chest and a pile of preprinted indulgence letters ready to be inscribed with the names of those who contributed. Martin Luther found such display and rhetoric offensive to his own struggle concerning salvation and fatal to genuine Christian piety.

Luther considered the question of indulgences as soon as he heard reports of Tetzel's preaching. Frederick the Wise, the Saxon elector, did not allow Tetzel to sell indulgences in his territory because they would compete with his own indulgences. Frederick collected relics enthusiastically—the 1518 catalog of his relics, which used woodcuts by Cranach, listed around 17,000 items—and displayed them in the castle church every year. The people of Wittenberg would view and pray before the relics in order to earn an indulgence. But the people considered the indulgences being sold by Tetzel more powerful and more easily obtained than the elector's, and so they traveled to adjacent territories to buy them. In the spring of 1517 they began to ask Luther as their priest to absolve them on the basis of the indulgence and without further penance. Luther responded by preaching sermons against indulgences and seeking out the opinion of church lawyers on the practice of indulgence sales.

By October 1517 Luther had formed his opinion concerning indulgences, and especially Tetzel's indulgence preaching. He penned the 95 *Theses* not only as an invitation to debate but also as a plea to Albrecht of Mainz to reexamine the methods of his indulgence sale. Although the theses tend to defy a simple analysis, three broad categories of Luther's concern can be identified. The theses express, first of all, Luther's understanding of penance as it relates to indulgences. The very first states, "When our Lord and Master Jesus Christ said, 'Repent,' he willed the entire life of the believer to be one of repentance." As Luther explained in the second thesis, the repentance Christ preached meant much more than doing the penances assigned by the priest. He used the Greek text of the New Testament to make the point that repentance meant not the sacrament but a change of mind and heart. For Luther, indulgences fostered a mechanical understanding of repentance that undermined the biblical teaching. Real Christians, he thought, would gladly do penance out of sorrow for their sin rather than pay to be free of such works. "A Christian who is truly contrite," he stated in Thesis 40, "seeks and loves to pay penalties for his sins." Second, Luther called into question the belief that theses could be purchased on behalf of a soul in purgatory, freeing that soul to enter heaven. This common belief preached by Tetzel, "When the coin in the coffer rings, the soul from purgatory springs," which Luther quoted in Thesis 27, became the object of his scorn in Thesis 28: "It is certain that when money clinks in the money chest, greed and avarice can be increased." The observation about souls in purgatory led Luther to put forth a more restrictive view of the pope's power. The theses argued that the pope could remit only those penalties that he had imposed (Thesis 5: "The pope neither desires or is able to remit any penalties except those imposed by his own authority or that of the canons.") and that, in any case, souls in purgatory were beyond his jurisdiction (Thesis 13: "The dying are freed by death from all penalties . . . and have a right to be released from them."). Third, Luther described indulgences, or at least trust in them, as detrimental to genuine Christian living. He would rather see the money used for indulgences spent on the poor and the time people spent in acquiring indulgences spent in prayer instead. (Thesis 43: "Christians are to be taught that he who gives to the poor or lends to the needy does a better deed than he who buys indulgences."; Thesis 48: "Christians are to be taught that the pope . . . needs and thus desires their devout prayer more than their money.") He applied the same logic to the pope's own actions in a way that, as we will see, fueled a negative reaction to the theses.

The theses were sent to Archbishop Albrecht as promulgator of the indulgence and to Bishop Jerome of Brandenburg as Luther's superior in the church. In the letter to Albrecht, Luther criticized the instructions for the indulgence sale but also assumed that Albrecht had not supervised their composition closely. Then on October 31 Luther also, it is commonly believed, nailed a copy of the theses to the door of the castle church in Wittenberg, which door served as the university bulletin board. (Melanchthon's biography of Luther, penned after Luther's death, provides the first account of attaching the theses to the church door. This was, however, a common enough practice that there is little reason to quibble about whether or not it happened.) Luther discussed the theses in letters to his friend Johann Lang in Erfurt and to Staupitz, but no one came forward to debate indulgences.

The matter might have ended there had it not been for the German printing industry. Recognizing that a wider public would be interested in Luther's attack on indulgences, printers copied and sold a German translation of the theses without his knowledge or consent. Printing with movable type was a relatively new technology at the time, and although Luther had used the local Wittenberg printer to prepare classroom materials, he had not yet witnessed the power of the press. He was not entirely happy about the almost miraculous speed with which his theses circulated. Yet the printing of the theses is a fitting first example of how printers helped to spread the ideas of the Reformation.

The theses made Luther famous or infamous, depending on your point of view, only because of the origin of this particular indulgence sale and because of the political situation in Germany. Concerned church leaders had routinely criticized the practices of the indulgence preachers. The theology faculty of the University of Paris had recorded its opposition to the idea that a monetary payment could release a soul from purgatory, and Cardinal Cajetan, who would later represent the pope in a meeting with Luther at Augsburg, called for a more precise definition of indulgences. So what Luther said was not entirely unique. The way he said it, however, drew attention to the sort of criticism of the pope that was quite common in Germany. He contrasted, for example, the wealth of the papacy with the poverty of many who bought indulgences. "Christians are to be taught," he wrote in Thesis 51, "that the pope would and should give of his own money, even though he had to sell the basilica of St. Peter [which was being built with the indulgence proceeds], to many of those from whom certain hawkers of indulgences cajole money." He also reported in the theses what he called the "slander or . . . shrewd questions of the laity." For example, Thesis 82 asked, "Why does not the pope empty purgatory for the sake of holy love . . . [rather than] for the sake of miserable money with which to build a church?"

As a result, many roundly condemned Luther for what appeared to be an attack on papal authority in the theses. Tetzel boasted, "In three weeks I will throw the heretic into the fire." He composed a set of counter-theses, some 800 copies of which were burned by Wittenberg university students. Archbishop Albrecht tempered his response out of fear of rousing Luther's Augustinian order against himself. The most surprising of the early attacks on Luther came from the Ingolstadt university professor Johann Eck. Luther had previously considered Eck a friend, but now the latter published a work entitled *Obelisks* that charged Luther with opposing papal authority. An obelisk was the sign commonly used at the time to mark heretical statements in a text. Luther titled his response to Eck

Asterisks, for the sign used to mark the most valuable statements in a text. Eck's attack would lead eventually to a disputation with Luther on papal authority. In the meantime, Luther was denounced to Rome and legal proceedings against him began in summer 1518. Under press of circumstances, Luther had continued to explain his understanding of indulgences. He preached on the topic in German and wrote his *Explanations of the Ninety-Five Theses*. But he also moved on to other issues and deepened and widened his critique of the medieval tradition. So we now turn to a pivotal moment in his rejection of the methods of scholastic theology.

The Heidelberg Disputation and the Critique of Scholasticism

The Augustinian order held one of its regular chapter meetings in Heidelberg in April 1518, a time of tension and uncertainty because of the unfolding controversy over indulgences. Whether or not Luther would need to give an answer concerning his attack on indulgences was unclear. He attended the meeting with Elector Frederick's promise that he would not be sent to Rome for trial. Despite his uncertain status, Luther was to be featured prominently at the chapter as the author of theses for a disputation. Staupitz, who gave him this task, also instructed him to avoid the topic of indulgences and present another issue for debate.

Luther continued an attack on scholastic theology he had begun the previous year in the theses he wrote for Heidelberg. Thesis 50 of his *Disputation against Scholastic Theology* (1517) stated, "The whole Aristotle is to theology as darkness is to light. This in opposition to the scholastics." In other theses of this disputation, Luther opposed those scholastics by name—William of Ockham, Pierre d'Ailly, and Gabriel Biel—and championed the theology of Augustine. Similar criticisms surfaced in the philosophical portion of the Heidelberg theses (Theses 29–40), but in the theological portion (Theses 1–28) Luther expanded his criticism of the scholastic understanding of righteousness along the lines of his previous lectures on Romans. He wrote in Thesis 3, "Although the works of man always seem attractive and good, they are nevertheless likely to be mortal sins." By this he meant that trusting in one's own works rather than in God was deadly. When in the subsequent thesis Luther called the works of God unattractive and evil by way of contrast, he meant the fact that God's law actually condemns the righteousness that humans try to achieve by themselves. He went on to accuse the scholastics of rejecting what God had said in Scripture and being "puffed up, blinded, and hardened" by their own way of trying to understand God. Luther identified himself, and others like him, as "theologians of the cross" who limited their understanding to what God had clearly revealed. Thus in the Heidelberg theses Luther stepped publicly beyond the criticism of indulgences toward a thorough reform of theology and theological method.

Although the Heidelberg disputation would seem to involve only the internal affairs of the German Augustinians, two aspects critical to the Reformation can be demonstrated from its aftermath. First, several men who would help to spread Luther's ideas and become reformers in their own right heard him first at Heidelberg. For example, Martin Bucer, at the time a Dominican who would later labor for reform in Strasbourg and England, wrote to Beatus Rhenanus, a fellow humanist, about "Martin, he of the indulgences" in debate at Heidelberg. According to Bucer, Luther agreed with Erasmus, the famed biblical humanist and classical scholar, but "taught openly and freely" what Erasmus insinuated. Second, at the time of the disputation and along the lines of thinking expressed there, Luther and his colleagues at Wittenberg had begun reforming the university to exclude Aristotle and scholasticism and to embrace those studies that would support their understanding of the gospel. That meant an emphasis on study of the Bible and of the languages in which it was originally written and also of more diverse topics such as history. Such studies had already been emphasized by a number of Christian humanists, and many humanists who had come to the cause of reforming the church through Erasmus and his writings heartily supported the developments in Wittenberg. The arrival of Philipp Melanchthon in August 1519 represented significant progress toward humanist reform at the university. Melanchthon, an academic prodigy and full-fledged humanist, had come to teach Greek, lacking as a field of study in medieval universities, and eventually took over Luther's lectures on Romans. (Melanchthon means *black earth* in Greek. Philipp, following a practice common among humanists, adopted this name to replace his German cognomen that had the same meaning, Schwartzerd.) Melanchthon would become the most trusted of Luther's Wittenberg colleagues and one of the great theologians of the Reformation.

The Leipzig Disputation and the Question of Authority

In July 1519 Martin Luther debated Johann Eck in Leipzig on the subject of the origin of papal authority. But it was not Luther who began the argument with Eck that provoked the Leipzig Disputation. That distinction belonged to Luther's colleague at the University of Wittenberg, Andreas Karlstadt. Eck and Luther had hoped to keep their exchange of treatises in the wake of the indulgence controversy a private matter, but Karlstadt received a copy of Eck's *Obelisks* and, on behalf of the entire University of Wittenberg, took offense at the attack. Karlstadt replied with his own set of theses, which he proposed to debate in the summer of 1518. This debate never took place. Instead, throughout the summer, Eck, Luther, and Karlstadt himself all attempted at various times to downplay the situation, but the damage had been done. In August, on the title page of a response to Karlstadt, Eck challenged him to a debate to be judged, he hoped, by the pope and the universities of Rome, Paris, or Cologne—an expression of Eck's confidence in his opinions and in his skill as a debater.

Eck arranged for the University of Leipzig to host the disputation, despite the faculty's reluctance to do anything that might provoke the neighboring Saxon elector. The elector's cousin Duke George of Saxony, the ruler of the territory that included Leipzig, had no such qualms and eagerly made the necessary arrangements. When Eck prepared the theses he wished to debate, it became clear that his real opponent was Luther rather than Karlstadt. Luther agreed to a debate and composed his own theses to counter Eck's. Luther's dramatic Thesis 13 would become the centerpiece of the debate, and even his friends found its wording extreme.

> 13. The very callous decrees of the Roman pontiffs which have appeared in the last four hundred years prove that the Roman church is superior to all others. Against them stand the history of eleven hundred years, the text of divine Scripture, and the decree of the Council of Nicaea, the most sacred of all councils.

Despite the fact that Luther entered the literary fray, Duke George, for reasons that he did not make clear, delayed in granting his permission for Luther to debate. So Luther arrived in Leipzig in June 1519 still uncertain about whether he would face Eck or not. Karlstadt, Luther, and the other professors from Wittenberg rode into Leipzig in carts, accompanied by about two hundred armed students from Wittenberg. As the group entered the city, Karlstadt was injured in a fall from his wagon when its wheel broke. In spite of his injury, Karlstadt negotiated with Eck, as did Luther—who would be allowed to participate—about the format for the debate. Eck proposed an "anything goes" Italian style that would favor his abilities, but the participants eventually settled on a more formal and sedate style.

On Monday, June 27 Eck and Karlstadt began to debate in the courtroom of Pleissenburg castle, because the University of Leipzig had no room large enough to accommodate the crowd. By most accounts, this portion of the debate was lackluster; everyone considered the matchup between Luther and Eck on the question of papal authority, scheduled for the beginning of July, to be the main event. Luther and Eck had announced their positions both in print and in the pulpit prior to the debate. So when they began the debate on July 4, their opening statements came as no surprise. Luther asserted that the pope had his authority by human arrangement rather than by divine right. He did not yet argue against the pope's authority or against the need for unity in the church, but he could not find the institution of the papacy in Scripture. As for the church fathers, Luther argued that more could be cited against divine institution than for it. Eck disagreed, saying that Luther had mangled his sources, and he repeated the accusation already made against Luther that his statements on the church came from the heretic Jan Hus. The charge would be devastating if it could be made to stick. Not only had Hus been declared a heretic by the general council of the church meeting in Constance and been executed by fire in that city in 1415, his Bohemian followers, the Hussites, had gone to war in defense of his ideas. Their armies had penetrated as far as Leipzig, and during the debate Duke George reacted angrily to Eck's mention of Hus.

So Luther was on the defensive. "First," he said, "I protest the affront that the learned lord doctor [Eck] charges me as zealous for and wholly a defender of the Bohemian faction (may the Lord spare him), particularly before such an audience as that gathered here." Luther attempted to deflect Eck's charge by observing that the Bohemians who had broken fellowship with Rome might be heretics, but the Greek Christians, who had not been officially in fellowship with Rome since 1054, most certainly were not. "Therefore," he continued, "if the divine right [of Rome] had existed for so long a time, all the bishops of Alexandria,

Constantinople, a number of whom were very holy men such as Gregory of Nazianzus and others, are damned, heretics and Bohemians. It is not possible to say anything more detestable than such blasphemy." Later in the day, Luther continued his defense: "I am certain that neither the Roman pope nor all his flatterers are able, under the power of the Roman popes or of their agents, to cast down from heaven such a great number of saints [i.e., of the Greek church]."

But Eck would not be so easily distracted. He pushed the point that Hus had been condemned by the Council of Constance, that is, by an authority that was normally accepted even by those who disputed concerning papal power. Luther had said that he found some of Hus's statements condemned by the council to be "plainly most Christian and evangelical." Although Luther interrupted Eck to deny that he had spoken against the council, Eck continued, observing that "the authority of the Council or the Roman popes is such that [Luther] is not able to defend what he has said without suspicion of heresy." Eventually Luther confessed his belief that councils were not infallible.

> I agree with the lord doctor that the statutes of the councils in those things that concern the faith ought to be honored in every way. I reserve for myself this alone, which indeed must be reserved, that a council has erred at times and is able to err at any time, especially in those things that do not concern the faith. Nor does a council have authority to establish new articles of faith, otherwise we would have as many such articles as there are human opinions.

Luther, with these words, severed his final connection to medieval conceptions of church authority. Although the popes had gradually exercised greater authority in the course of the Middle Ages, they had also been challenged by conciliarists—those who had come to believe that a general council wielded a higher authority than that of the popes. Nor was canon law, the collection of the decisions and rules of popes and councils, unambiguous concerning the extent of papal authority. For Luther to champion the general council against the pope could be an acceptable position, especially in Germany where conciliar sentiment lingered well into the sixteenth century.

The Leipzig debate served further to divide opinion about Luther. He had persuaded some but not others. Many would have gladly shaken off papal authority but were not yet convinced it would be possible. During the debate Duke George himself observed one day at breakfast, "Whether by divine or human right, nevertheless he is pope." Others who criticized individual popes and the practices of the papal church were not prepared to reject the papacy as an institution or to attempt to unify the church with Scripture alone. Following the debate Eck's opposition to Luther intensified, the Universities of Louvain and Cologne condemned him, and new opponents entered the fray on the pope's behalf. But Luther had made friends with his position at well. Among these were, of course, the Bohemians. One Bohemian professor sent copies of Hus's works to Luther, who adopted a much more favorable view of Hus than he had held at Leipzig. By 1520 Luther was able to write in a letter, "I have previously been teaching everything that Hus taught and believed without knowing it . . . unawares, we are all Hussites." Little wonder, then, that Luther's trial for heresy had been proceeding at Rome in the meantime.

The Beginning of Luther's Papal Trial

Luther had spent the summer of 1518, a year before Leipzig, waiting for Rome's response to the indulgence controversy. In August he received the summons to Rome to answer charges of heresy and, along with the summons, a work identifying his errors composed by the pope's court theologian, Sylvester Prierias. Luther demonstrated his lack of intellectual humility by composing a response to Prierias in two days, noting that the matter was worth no more of his time than that. Yet he also expressed alarm at the summons. He continued to believe, or at least hope, that the pope himself had not prejudged him and would agree with his criticisms of the excesses of the indulgence preachers.

Only the Augustinian order or Elector Frederick could force Luther to obey the summons. Even Rome recognized the futility of asking Staupitz, Luther's superior in the Augustinian order, to hand him over—the Augustinian authorities there wrote to another German Augustinian official instead. So when the summons came, the Wittenberg professor's future depended on the goodwill of his sovereign. Because Frederick, as one of the electors, was an important official in the Holy Roman Empire, Luther's case immediately became caught up in imperial politics. The elector seemed inclined to protect his star professor and had refused to listen to Eck's accusations against him. Frederick, like many other rulers, did not fear the pope excessively—in many ways the pope functioned and was treated as another secular ruler. Frederick, for example, opposed the pope's plan to impose a tax on the Germans in order to fund a war against the Turks. The possibility remained that Frederick would bow to pressure from the emperor himself. But the emperor needed Frederick's support for his plan to be succeeded in office by his grandson, Charles I of Spain. As a result of this impending election in which his vote would be needed, Elector Frederick could successfully fight a delaying action on Luther's behalf.

Frederick negotiated, as a first move, for Luther to be interviewed by Cardinal Cajetan in Augsburg. Both the elector and the cardinal, as the pope's appointed representative, were in Augsburg for a Diet, or meeting, of the Holy Roman Empire. When the Diet concluded, Luther traveled to Augsburg to meet with Cajetan rather than going to Rome. Although Cajetan had not seemed to Frederick to be unfriendly toward Luther, the series of meetings held in Augsburg did not go well. Cajetan, who had been instructed by the pope not to engage Luther in debate, nevertheless debated papal authority with him. Luther, for his part, could not resist the temptation to display his mastery of the sources in front of the cardinal. Although in his own account of the meetings Luther emphasized his respectful demeanor, he also reports how he contradicted Cajetan's statements in praise of papal authority. For example, Cajetan had identified Luther as a conciliarist and so emphasized to him that believing in the superiority of general councils had been condemned by the pope. Luther responded by denying that the pope was superior to a council and expressed surprise at the novelty of Cajetan's opinion. Cajetan had insisted that Luther recant, to which demand the professor responded in writing. Amidst the usual protestations of submission to the church Luther declared his position.

I, who debated and sought the truth could not have done wrong by such inquiry, much less be compelled to retract unheard or unconvinced. Today I declare publicly that I am not conscious of having said anything contrary to Holy Scripture, the church fathers, or papal decretals or their correct meaning. All that I have said today seems to me to have been sensible, true, and catholic.

Clearly Luther and Cajetan were talking past each other. The cardinal promoted the pope's authority. The professor countered with his right to debate and his need to be convinced by the evidence.

Before he left Augsburg Luther lodged a formal legal appeal that asked the pope himself to further investigate the case before judging him. Although Luther might still have believed the pope would rule in his favor, he lodged the appeal on the advice of Elector Frederick's lawyers as a delaying tactic. Luther also sent a letter to Cajetan apologizing for any offense he might have given in his speech. But Cajetan was not mollified and, in October 1518, sent a letter to Frederick demanding that he send Luther to Rome. Frederick requested a response from Luther, which he provided, and then Luther waited anxiously to discover the elector's intention. At the same time, Luther lodged a formal appeal from the pope as judge in his case to a general council of the church. This maneuver would buy him no time in Rome, since the pope had forbidden such appeals, but might help to rouse public opinion in his favor because many influential people in Germany held the authority of a council in higher regard than that of the pope. In December Frederick replied to Cajetan's demand. The elector stated unequivocally that he would not surrender Luther until his case had been discussed sufficiently and he had been convicted of heresy.

In that same month a papal ambassador, Karl von Miltitz, arrived in Wittenberg. Miltitz was a German nobleman serving at the papal court who was convinced that he could succeed in negotiating with Elector Frederick and Luther where others had failed. He was prepared, with the pope's blessing, to persuade the elector to cooperate by flattery rather than by force. He came to present Frederick with the "Golden Rose of Virtue," a papal award for princes in the form of a rose made out of gold. When Miltitz met with Luther early in January 1519, he explained that he considered Tetzel as culpable in the controversy as Luther. Luther, in an attempt at compromise that might seem uncharacteristic in light of his meeting with Cajetan, offered to keep silent if his opponents would do the same and to write a letter of apology to the pope. But Luther refused to utter the words *I recant*. In the middle of January Emperor Maximilian died. Elector Frederick, who would serve as imperial vicar until a new emperor was elected, would now be free from papal pressure in the Luther affair. The pope needed his vote to enthrone someone other than Charles of Spain. If Charles became Holy Roman Emperor as well as King of Spain, he would rule outright or have a claim to territory that completely surrounded the Papal States. The pope was not on friendly enough terms with the empire to allow that to happen if he could help it. So while Luther debated in Leipzig he was, for the moment, shielded from papal and imperial coercion. How he would be declared a heretic is discussed in Chapter 3.

Writing History: The Date of Luther's Breakthrough

This chapter described Luther's breakthrough without giving a precise date for this important moment because scholars disagree profoundly about when the breakthrough actually took place and even about exactly what it was. Luther did not write his own account of the breakthrough until 1545 as part of the preface to a collection of his early works. In this text (see callout selection in Chapter 1), he states, "Meanwhile in that year [1519] I returned a second time to the interpretation of the Psalms." After this he explains his discovery concerning the phrase *the righteousness of God*. Although the grammar of this passage is somewhat ambiguous, Luther seems to suggest that his breakthrough moment came around 1519. He described the same experience to his companions at table on three separate occasions between 1532 and 1543 but without adding any precision to the date. In the 1532 version he said it took place "in the tower" (i.e., the tower of the Augustinian monastery in Erfurt that the elector had given to Luther for his residence), so the breakthrough is also sometimes called "the tower experience." In another version Luther described the breakthrough in a way that might indicate he was in the lavatory. (This version involves an abbreviation in the manuscript that is in some dispute. The interested reader should consult *Luther's Works* 54:193, note 65.) Because, as we have seen, Luther used language that is strikingly similar to his 1545 account of the breakthrough before 1519, scholars have expressed uncertainty about when to date that breakthrough.

Karl Holl, one of the scholars of the "Luther Renaissance" (a renewal of interest in historical study of Luther) of the early twentieth century, provides an example of an early dating for the breakthrough. Holl accepted Luther's account of the content of the discovery but believed that Luther must have been mistaken about the date. Because Luther appears to express his understanding of the righteousness of God long before 1519, Holl believed that the tower experience had taken place before Luther's first Psalms lectures. Ernst Bizer, on the other hand, has argued for the 1519 date, believing that Luther's breakthrough consisted of a more radical reliance on the righteousness of God through faith alone, with a great emphasis on *alone*. The emphasis on faith alone is, according to Bizer, lacking in Luther's thought before 1519. As might be expected, many other scholars take a mediating position by distinguishing in some fashion between the "tower experience" and the beginning of Luther's turn toward a reformed understanding of salvation. Uuras Saarnivaara, for example, distinguished two moments in Luther's understanding. First, he began to understand righteousness and faith. This happened early on under Staupitz's tutelage. Second, Luther achieved genuine certainty about his understanding of righteousness after years of studying and lecturing. Thus what he described as his breakthrough marked the end rather than the beginning of a process of discovery.

The discussion surrounding the date of the breakthrough illustrates how historians work with the information at hand. In this case, Luther's own comment from 1545 poses a potential problem when compared with his early writings. When the event Luther described took place depends on what we think he understood by that event. In other words, if his 1545 remark refers only to a new understanding of the phrase *the righteousness of God* based on its grammar, then we must date the breakthrough before 1519. If, however, Luther meant that he had discovered genuine certainty and confidence in his interpretation of *the righteousness of God*, then a later date is more than possible.

When the breakthrough moment occurred can make a difference in how we read Luther's earliest writings. If we believe the breakthrough came after the *95 Theses*, for example, the theses might appear to be the somewhat naïve remarks of a concerned professor. Or, if Luther was at the time confident in his understanding of righteousness and faith, the theses could be a more calculated blow against the theology of the Roman Church. In spite of the number of books already written about Luther and the number of surviving pages written by Luther, such questions remain to be analyzed and debated. Yet whatever date we accept for the breakthrough, by the end of 1519 Luther had reformed himself from questioning scholar to confident reformer.

Luther in His Own Words: A Selection from the Leipzig Disputation

A key section of the Leipzig Disputation, described in this chapter, is presented more completely here. It is July 5, 1519, and Luther is responding to the charge of his opponent, Johann Eck, that he is repeating the heresy of Jan Hus and the Hussites. In his defense, Luther appeals to early church history, to the example of the Greek (Byzantine Orthodox) Church that had formally and officially separated from the Roman Church in 1054, and to the text of Scripture as a greater authority than the early church fathers.

First I protest the affront that the learned lord doctor charges me as zealous for and wholly a defender of the Bohemian faction (may the Lord spare him), and I protest particularly that he does it in front of such an audience as is gathered here. Schism of any kind never has been nor ever will be pleasing to me. The Bohemians do evil because by their own authority they separate from our unity, even if the divine law is on their side, because the highest divine law is charity and unity of spirit. I have sought this only and I ask any good Christian that he consent to ponder in Christian charity whether it is not a long-standing, shameless act of unfairness to have cast out of the church so many thousands of martyrs and saints who had been within the Greek church for one thousand four hundred years and now even to pluck out and cast down those who are reigning in heaven. For even if all the flatterers of the Roman pontiffs are insane, they are not able to deny that the church of Christ, gathered from many parts of the world, had been founded for twenty years before Peter founded the Roman church. This is most clearly shown by the Epistle to the Galatians where Paul writes that he had come to Peter after three years, then after fourteen years had gone up again to Peter.[1] If we compare these things, we find that they took place fully eighteen years after the ascension of Christ, when Peter was still at Jerusalem (granting that I am silent concerning the years he remained at Antioch) so that it is not possible to say that the Roman church is first and head by divine right. Now that fact urgently compels us [in the matter at hand] because the Greek Church up until our own time never accepted that its bishops be confirmed by Rome. Therefore if the divine right [of Rome] had existed for so long a time, all the bishops of Alexandria, Constantinople, a number of whom were very holy men such as Gregory of Nazianzus and others, are damned, heretics and Bohemians. It is not possible to say anything more detestable than such blasphemy.

Third [Dr. Eck] proved [his point] by those words: "You are Peter and upon this rock, etc." which Augustine expounded thus, "Upon this rock, that is Peter." And this he will not have withdrawn. I respond: What is it to me? If he wishes to fight against me, he must first himself reconcile contrary sayings. For it is certain that Augustine often expounded the rock as Christ and perhaps just a single time as Peter—again he does more for me than against me. Because even if Augustine and all the fathers have understood the rock to be Peter, I resist them as one by the authority of the apostle, that is by divine right, who wrote 1 Corinthians 3: "No one is able to lay another foundation than that which has been laid, which is Jesus Christ," and by the authority of 1 Peter 2, where Christ is called the living stone and cornerstone, teaching that we must be built upon him in a spiritual house. Otherwise if Peter is the foundation of the church, the church might have fallen by the word of a single doormaid,[2] which church the gates of hell will not be able to overcome. Therefore it follows that the holy fathers, when they call the rock Peter, in this place either are endured as human or have some other meaning concerning which I cannot pronounce.

---

[1] Galatians 1:18; 2:1.
[2] A reference to Peter denying that he knew Jesus when questioned by a doormaid during Jesus' trial before the high priest.

3

The Reformer (1520–1521)

Introduction

"I am bound by the Scriptures I have quoted and my conscience is captive to the Word of God. I cannot and I will not retract anything, since it is neither safe nor right to go against conscience. I cannot do otherwise, here I stand, may God help me. Amen." This final portion of Luther's answer to Emperor Charles V in 1521 offers a fitting prelude to an account of the reformer's activities in the 1520s. Through a turbulent decade, a "conscience captive to the Word of God" drove Martin Luther the reformer.

1520: Luther Establishes Himself as a Reformer

Martin Luther emerged fully and formally as a reformer of the church in the year 1520. Early in that year it became clear that those in the church hierarchy who wanted Luther condemned as a heretic had the pope's ear. Luther became more radical in condemning the practices of the Roman church and also began to write about how the church should be reformed as a result of his understanding of the gospel. By the summer of 1520 he was writing some of the most significant reformatory treatises of his career. In the same year King Charles I of Spain, who had been elected Holy Roman Emperor in the previous year, made slow and stately progress toward his coronation. The political considerations of emperor and empire would add another dimension to Luther's official standing and to the shape of his career as a reformer.

Pope Leo X formed a committee to reconsider charges against Luther in February of 1520. During the previous year the pope had been unwilling to move against Luther. At first Leo had been working against the election of Charles of Spain as Holy Roman Emperor and could not afford to alienate Luther's prince and protector, Frederick of Saxony, who was one of the electors. Even after the electors chose Charles in June 1519, the pope had to deal carefully with Frederick and authorized Karl von Miltitz to attempt negotiations with Frederick and Luther. By the beginning of 1520 negotiations seemed to have failed and Luther's opponents in the church hierarchy called for his condemnation. One of these opponents was Cardinal Cajetan, who now chaired the committee that would examine Luther's writings for heresy. In the meantime the universities of Louvain and Cologne had condemned certain of Luther's propositions, and Cajetan's committee used these condemnations as the basis of its report. Cajetan proposed that the committee draft a letter to Luther demanding, once again, that he recant. Johann Eck, another of Luther's opponents who had been urging the pope to condemn him, considered this letter a far too tepid response. Eck undertook to chair another committee that compiled a list of Luther's errors. Using the work of Eck's committee, the cardinals, who served as the pope's advisors in such matters, agreed to condemn forty-one statements from Luther's various writings.

Once Luther's ideas had been condemned, the cardinals had to decide what to do about the man himself. The theologians among them believed that Luther had already condemned himself by authoring heresy; the lawyers among them, and there were many, believed it irregular to condemn someone without a hearing. Because the lawyers and the theologians agreed that Luther was unlikely to come to Rome to defend himself, they reached a compromise. They drafted a document listing Luther's errors and stating that he would be condemned unless he recanted within sixty days of receiving a copy. This bull (named for the lead seals that were attached to such documents—*bulla* in Latin) was titled *Exsurge Domine*, after the first words of the text: "Arise, O Lord." The first paragraph of the bull emphasizes the pope's position as successor to Peter and compares the church to a vineyard that the wild boar Luther is trying to destroy.

> Arise, O Lord, and judge your own cause. Remember your reproaches to those who are filled with foolishness all through the day. Listen to our prayers, for foxes have arisen seeking to destroy the vineyard whose winepress you alone have trod. When you were about to ascend to your Father, you committed the care, rule, and administration of the vineyard, an image of the triumphant church, to Peter, as the head and your vicar and his successors. The wild boar from the forest seeks to destroy it and every wild beast feeds upon it.

The pope proclaimed the bull officially on June 15, 1520. Johann Eck and Jerome Aleander accepted the task of publicizing the bull in Germany. Eck agreed to go to Luther's own territory of Electoral Saxony, whose ruler, Frederick, was threatened with condemnation by the bull along with his famous professor, Luther.

Luther realized that he faced stiff opposition from Eck and that he had few defenders in Rome. Already in December 1519 he had confided in a letter that Eck was threatening even Elector Frederick in such a way that "you would have thought Almighty God himself was speaking." Luther knew what was at stake and that he differed with the Roman church on important issues, but he had also agreed to keep silent for the sake of peace in the church. He would not maintain that silence for long. By the summer of 1520 he was prepared to unleash devastating criticism on the papacy and its teachings.

Luther attacked the papal office, and specifically what he considered its presumption of universal rule, after an obscure Franciscan friar had published a treatise correcting his view of the papacy. Luther thought little of the Franciscan's style or logic but felt compelled to reply. Even the title of the reply—*On the Papacy*

Against the Most Celebrated Romanist in Leipzig—mocked his opponent by calling him a "most celebrated Romanist," that is, a distinguished defender of the papacy. The treatise itself disparages the friar's arguments and reiterates Luther's proposition at Leipzig that the pope could claim no power over the church by divine right. He based this argument, as he had at Leipzig, on history and Scripture. His historical argument is that the pope never ruled over all of Christendom. Peter did not rule the other apostles, and throughout history people who were clearly Christian had existed apart from papal rule. Luther's argument from Scripture advanced the case beyond what he had already argued against Eck in Leipzig—not that he or his opponent had discovered any new passages in the biblical text concerning the papacy. Luther, because he now considered himself bound only by the words of Scripture, rejected arguments for papal authority from any other source, including the church fathers. Along with this sole reliance on Scripture came his insistence that it be interpreted correctly. Luther demanded, as had theologians throughout the Middle Ages, that in matters of church teaching the plain sense of a passage had to be used. He would not allow passages to be interpreted figuratively or metaphorically, as his Franciscan opponent had done, in defense of papal power.

Luther concluded his treatise by stating that he was willing to accept the pope's rule as something established by God, but only in the same way that God, according to Scripture, had established all governments. Luther suggested that everyone should "honor such power, and endure it with all patience, just as though the Turks ruled over us." He had every intention of insulting the papacy and those who supported it when he compared papal rule to that of the Turk, since the Turks were at the time the greatest enemies of Christian Europe. Furthermore, Luther narrowly circumscribed the pope's governing power by stating clearly that he had no right to establish new teachings and that everything he did was subject to judgment based on Scripture. In other words, Luther rejected the pope's spiritual authority but accepted his temporal authority—precisely the opposite of the situation of the papacy today. Yet this was a trajectory that the popes themselves had established in the later fifteenth century. The general councils of the church that met in the first half of the fifteenth century not only solved the schism—a time when there were two and then three competing popes—but also tried to curtail papal power. The popes traded power over the local churches to the kings and princes of Europe in exchange for their support against the councils. In the second half of the century, the popes immersed themselves in politics and refashioned themselves as Italian princes concerned with the aggrandizement of the Papal States. As a result, European princes, such as Elector Frederick of Saxony, frequently dealt with the popes as fellow rulers rather than as spiritual leaders. So, too, Luther could affirm that the pope's temporal rule was as legitimate as that of any other monarch, but his spiritual rule was unacceptable. According to Luther, numerous other reformers, and much public opinion, the pope had ceased to fulfill his spiritual duties as Bishop of Rome. Luther declared in *On the Papacy* that the pope and his supporters boasted about being shepherds but were really wolves.

Such rhetoric aside, neither Luther nor his opponents fully recognized the extent to which they were arguing past each other. The fundamental issue between them was not the papacy as such but the more general question of authority in the church. Was church teaching to be based solely on Scripture, as Luther maintained, or on some combination of Scripture and tradition (whether that meant the church fathers, the councils of the church, or the popes), as his opponents insisted? Because Luther and his opponents did not agree on how to answer this question, they had very little common ground in their debates. Both sides employed arguments that the other would reject from the outset. As the formal legal case against him advanced, Luther continued to insist that his teachings be judged by Scripture alone. And his opponents would continue to wonder how he could expect such a novel approach.

Luther published *On the Papacy* on June 11, 1520—four days before the pope proclaimed the bull threatening his condemnation. Martin Luther and Pope Leo X had drawn their lines in the sand. The remainder of that year would see a host of intricate maneuvers between the two camps as the pope attempted to gather support for Luther's condemnation and Luther himself made his case for the reform of the church in three remarkable treatises. In these treatises, Luther laid out who should reform the church, what needed to be reformed, and why reform was necessary. The first to appear, *An Appeal to the Christian Nobility of the German Nation*, answered the question of who should reform the church. Luther acknowledged that this duty fell to the bishops, but he encouraged the rulers of the German territories to reform the church in their lands if the bishops refused to do so. The second treatise, *Prelude on the Babylonian Captivity of the Church*, attacked the sacramental system of the medieval church. Luther argued that instead of the seven sacraments that had become traditional in the Middle Ages there should, according to Scripture, be only two or three. He also opposed the medieval understanding that the church controlled the sacraments. In the third treatise, *On the Freedom of a Christian*, Luther articulated his understanding of two kinds of righteousness in terms of the Christian's freedom from law in matters of salvation and the Christian's duty to serve others. Together these three texts demonstrate the key ideas undergirding Luther's understanding of church reform.

To the Christian Nobility demonstrates the extent to which the German political situation and political issues had become entwined with the reform ideas Luther articulated. Luther himself had planned no such thing, but because the papacy was a political power, any attack on the pope could not help but be politicized. As a result, whatever Luther himself might say about his reasons for criticizing the papacy, others could always turn his criticisms to their own political gain. The German princes could certainly do so, and their political reality is critical to our understanding of *To the Christian Nobility*.

In 1520 King Charles I of Spain was making his way into Germany to be crowned Holy Roman Emperor of the German Nation. The various factions and powerful individuals within Germany apprehensively awaited his arrival. Some simply hoped that Charles would be a benign ruler; others decided that the time was ripe for change. Franz von Sickingen and Ulrich von Hutten, two powerful knights, decided to take the initiative to alter the German political landscape, and Luther was to be part of their plan. Von Sickingen had enough influence, and enough armed men at his disposal, that his approval had been sought before King Charles was elected emperor. Von Hutten, a humanist scholar as well as a knight, wielded a different kind of influence. His writings attempted to shape public opinion along the lines of a specifically German nationalism at the expense of the papacy. He and Luther agreed that the papacy was systematically destroying Germany. So when these two knights planned an armed uprising against Rome, they naturally expected Luther's enthusiastic participation. But when their emissary offered an army of knights for Luther's cause, the professor politely declined. When he later wrote *To the Christian Nobility*, he explicitly rejected any violence and wrote positively concerning the new emperor, "God has given us a young man of noble birth as head of state, and in him has awakened great hopes of good in many hearts."

Charles would require more than "great hopes of good" to rule the Empire effectively. In the early sixteenth century Germany existed as an idea but not as a politically unified state. The Holy Roman Empire of the German Nation consisted of hundreds of more or less autonomous territories ruled variously by princes, dukes, bishops, knights, and city councils. Emperor Maximilian I had tried to centralize and regularize governing institutions with only partial success. In fact, the princes and electors, rulers of the largest territories, had the upper hand in German politics. They had begun to take over smaller territories and would continue to do so at the expense of the lesser nobility and especially the knights. Members of this upper class of the German nobility were the power brokers, and even the emperor had to be careful in his dealings with them. Luther appealed particularly to this group in *To the Christian Nobility* because they had the authority and the means to enact his ideas for reform. Luther the reformer cast himself as counselor to the German princes.

The idea that the nobility should exercise control over the churches in their territories did not originate with Luther. The papacy and the princes of Europe had fought long and hard in the Middle Ages for control of the church. The papacy had gradually won an incomplete victory at significant cost. In Germany the so-called "proprietary church system," in which the ruler of a territory also ruled over the church there, had never been totally eradicated. Luther justified a return to this system by demolishing what he called three walls the papacy had built around itself: the idea that the pope was not subject to any temporal authority, that only the pope could interpret Scripture, and that only the pope could call a general council of the church. Luther is able to dismiss these ideas rather quickly and in the bulk of the treatise offer his suggestions for reform. He discusses twenty-five items that he believes should be dealt with by a church council. Few of these ideas were brand new, but Luther willingly pushed them to their limits. He also posited a complete equality of status between clergy and laity that struck even some other reformers as too radical. Erasmus, for example, criticized Luther for allowing everyone, not just scholars, to discuss and debate theology.

Luther was willing to speak the language of the princes if it would further his cause of reform. *To the Christian Nobility*, being written in German, spoke the princes' language literally, but Luther also went out of his way to demonstrate the advantages that would accrue to the German rulers if they freed themselves from the papacy. Not least of these would be retaining the tax money that flowed from Germany into the Roman coffers. Luther also intentionally employed harsh language to make his points. He reiterated a complaint common in Germany that Italian churchmen had themselves appointed to positions in Germany in order to add to their already large incomes. "The 'drunken Germans,' " wrote Luther, "are not supposed to understand what the Romanists are up to until there is not a bishopric, a monastery, a living, a benefice, not a red cent left." Not content to charge the pope with "avarice and robbery," Luther even suggested that the pope was the Antichrist, a figure who, according to Scripture, would arise to oppose Christ as the world draws to an end. Luther was criticized for the language he used in this treatise, and both his friends and his enemies would continue to shudder at the rhetoric he sometimes employed. Luther answered the criticism by pointing to the magnitude of his cause—St. Paul himself had called his enemies names in defense of the gospel! More important than the language Luther employed, however, is the new self-confidence he demonstrated. When before he had seemed, at least, to be a somewhat naïve and very careful university professor, he was now a reformer who expected even the princes to heed his diagnosis of the church's ills and embrace his remedies for them.

Dr. Luther made a further diagnosis, this one directed to the theologians, in the second key treatise of 1520, *Prelude on the Babylonian Captivity of the Church*. In this lengthy and complex treatise, Luther made a simple point. According to Scripture, there are only two or three sacraments and not seven as the medieval church had maintained. Luther would retain only baptism, the Lord's Supper (Mass), and possibly confession (penance) as sacraments. (He concluded, by the end of the treatise, that confession could really be considered to belong to baptism and, for that reason, could be considered a third sacrament or not.) Luther no longer regarded marriage, holy orders, extreme unction, and confirmation as sacraments. Showing a profound knowledge of the medieval tradition and also a sense of the church's history, Luther demonstrated how the current sacramental system had developed. His study of Scripture led him to the conclusion that God used sacraments to forgive sins. Only baptism and the Lord's Supper had God's own promise of forgiveness attached to them. In addition, even these sacraments had not been practiced as God had instituted them. The Roman church had turned them into good works to be done by Christians rather than seeing them as means through which God forgives sins. The reference in the title of the treatise to the Babylonian captivity—the time when the Old Testament Jews were exiled in Babylon for seventy years—reflects Luther's belief that the Roman church had used the sacraments to hold Christians captive under its authority.

With this seemingly simple conclusion Luther undermined much of medieval theology and piety. Nowhere was this more apparent than in his discussion of the Mass. In medieval theology, the Mass was primarily a sacrifice in which the priest offered up bread and wine that had become the body and blood of Christ. Because lay people normally received the sacrament once a year—and then received only the bread, also called the host, rather than both bread and wine—their focus had shifted to being present when the sacrifice was offered. The theologians agreed that people could receive grace by attending the Mass without receiving the bread. In addition, a number of other devotional practices sprang up around the Mass—from the veneration of particular hosts, such as the "bleeding hosts" of Wilsnack in Germany, to the popular festival of Corpus

Christi. (Corpus Christi is Latin for "the body of Christ." The festival included a procession with the hosts that had been kept aside after Mass was celebrated.) Luther's conclusions that the Mass was not a sacrifice, that Christ had meant for Christians to receive the bread *and* the wine, and that the main thing in this sacrament was forgiveness made practically every pious practice and theological statement concerning the Mass irrelevant. The thoughts he expressed in the *Prelude on the Babylonian Captivity* shocked some readers and captivated others. Luther clearly believed that his renewed understanding of the gospel would require drastic change to centuries of church teaching and practice.

Luther published *Prelude on the Babylonian Captivity of the Church* in October 1520, the same month in which Eck proclaimed the bull *Exsurge Domine* in Leipzig. Luther had printed treatise after treatise proclaiming his freedom from the pope's authority, and now the pope's representative publicly threatened him with excommunication. Yet at this moment when it might have seemed that a break between Luther and Rome was inevitable, Karl von Miltitz revived the idea of reconciling the two parties. Miltitz hoped to regain some of the glory he had lost because of the bull and reasoned that the pope would still welcome a diplomatic solution. Frederick the Wise, having lost much of his bargaining power with the pope now that a new emperor was about to be crowned, willingly accepted Miltitz's offer of mediation. Luther acquiesced. He was not certain how involved Pope Leo X himself had been in the process that resulted in the bull. In fact, Luther had responded in print to the bull as if he believed, or at least wished to believe, Eck had fabricated it. In this atmosphere, Miltitz hoped for a compromise. He met with Luther halfway between Wittenberg and Leipzig. At his urging Luther wrote a conciliatory letter to Pope Leo and added to it the third significant treatise to come from his pen in 1520, *The Freedom of a Christian.*

Conciliatory as the letter was—and Luther's words could be honeyed as well as harsh—it conceded not a single point to Rome. Instead, Luther addressed the pope as if his advisors had deceived him, likening him to Daniel in the den of lions and a sheep in the midst of wolves. Luther told Leo that he was "worthy of being pope in better times." The treatise attached to the letter, *The Freedom of a Christian*, extolled Christian freedom from laws when it came to salvation. Luther declared, "A Christian is a perfectly free lord of all subject to none." What he meant was that a true Christian relied for salvation on Christ alone rather than on human rules and laws, even those made by the pope. This is simply another way of explaining Luther's understanding of the righteousness given freely by God. Not even following biblical rules and laws could help someone save himself; Christ alone could save. Luther, nevertheless, considered rules and laws important for life in the world. He expressed this understanding of a Christian's active righteousness in the second major proposition of the treatise, "A Christian is a perfectly dutiful servant of all subject to all." The Christian was freed from doing things in order to be saved. So instead of going on pilgrimages and performing penances, Christian women and men could use that time and energy to do good works for their neighbors.

The Freedom of the Christian became one of Luther's most important and influential treatises. But the letter and the treatise were too little and too late to influence Rome. By the time they were printed, events had overtaken Miltitz's scheme. In any case, Pope Leo X was not a man to be impressed by anything less from Luther than a recantation and an acknowledgment of the sovereign authority of the papacy. Leo had survived a conspiracy by some of his own cardinals to kill him and could not have greatly feared a German monk and professor of theology from little Wittenberg. He should have been more concerned than he was. The cities of Germany did not all eagerly receive the bull against Luther from the hands of Aleander and Eck, the papal nuncios. Even the University of Leipzig, instrumental in the debate between Eck and Luther, would not allow Eck to post the bull. Eck sent a copy to the University of Wittenberg rather than delivering it in person. Aleander tried to catch up with Elector Frederick in Cologne, where he awaited the arrival of the emperor-elect. Frederick refused to receive the nuncio, who finally resorted to delivering the bull to the elector while he was attending Mass. Having failed to stave off the bull, Frederick asked for advice from the famed humanist reformer Erasmus, also in the city to meet the new emperor. Erasmus expressed support for Luther but was unwilling to commit himself until Frederick pressed him. Erasmus would concede that Luther had not been refuted and that the papal bull was worse than anything Luther had said.

Others, of course, stood more firmly in Luther's camp than did Erasmus. Because Luther's opponents had, with great ceremony, burned his books, the students at the University of Wittenberg gathered on the morning of December 10 to burn the books of the pope. The notice advertising the book burning, penned by Melanchthon, had concluded, "Come pious and studious young men, share in this pious and religious spectacle. For perhaps now is the time for the Antichrist to be revealed!" While the students fed the fire with books of church law and the works of medieval theologians, Martin Luther walked forward and added to the flames his copy of the bull *Exsurge Domine*. Profoundly conscious of the significance of his action, Luther explained himself first in the classroom and then in print. In a brief treatise written in German, he offered the reasons for his action, including his belief that Pope Leo was not personally responsible for the bull. But the most revealing of all the explanations Luther put forward is this: "I am, however unworthy, a baptized Christian, in addition a sworn doctor of Holy Scripture, and beyond that a preacher each weekday whose duty it is on account of his name, station, oath, and office, to destroy or at least to ward off false, corrupt, unchristian doctrine." Luther might have added that this understanding of himself and his office had made him a reformer.

As the year 1521 dawned, another papal bull concerning Luther appeared. This one condemned him as a heretic deserving the death sentence. The reaction from Wittenberg is best summarized in a series of woodcuts by Cranach published in the same year. These showed the actions of Christ contrasted with the actions of the pope as Antichrist. If Christ is shown refusing to be made king, for example, the pope is shown leading an army. Where Christ is shown driving salesmen out of the temple, the pope is shown collecting money. Finally, Christ ascends into heaven on one side and the pope is cast into hell on the other—a visual indication of the mood that prevailed among Luther's followers. Luther had laid out his program for reform and had gained a large following. He had succeeded in establishing himself as a reformer. It remained to be seen if he could keep himself alive.

The Imperial Diet of 1521 at Worms

King Charles I of Spain became Emperor Charles V in the cathedral of Aachen (also known as Aix-la-Chapelle) on October 23, 1520. After being crowned by the Archbishop of Cologne, he sat on Charlemagne's throne. Even before the ceremony Charles considered carefully how he might actually rule the empire along with his other territories. As we have noted, the Holy Roman Empire of the German Nation was more a loose federation of territories than a nation. The German princes did not wish to have a powerful emperor. Moreover, Charles had to rule over Germans without being German and without speaking their language, just as he had become King of Spain knowing no Spanish. Although he was the grandson of the former emperor, Charles had been raised in the Netherlands by his aunt. His father, the Duke of Burgundy, which territory at that time included the Netherlands, had died when he was six. Charles grew up speaking French, the language of the Burgundian court, and thinking of himself as a heroic knight. By the time he became emperor, Charles excelled at the joust and had ruled nations, first Burgundy and then, in addition, Spain, for five years.

Emperor Charles V, amidst a host of other problems, would have to deal with Martin Luther. Luther had been invited to appear at an upcoming meeting of the estates, that is, the clergy, the nobility, and the cities, of the Holy Roman Empire. The diet, as such meetings were known, was to be held in the city of Worms and would treat a host of other matters such as taxation and war against the Turks. Emperor Charles, however, withdrew Luther's invitation when the sixty days he was given to recant by *Exsurge Domine* expired. When the diet opened in January, Luther was no longer on the agenda, but some of the German rulers continued to push for Luther to appear. As far as they were concerned, the papal condemnation had not spoken the final word on Luther. Many in Germany would consider him duly condemned only when a general council of the church pronounced that sentence. Through negotiations between the Chancellor of Saxony and Emperor Charles's confessor, Father Glapion, the emperor agreed to honor his original promise not to condemn Luther unheard, no doubt because he realized that many in Germany still favored Luther.

Luther, indeed, traveled to Worms for his audience in heroic style. Cheering crowds greeted him along the way and people thronged to the churches where he preached. Glapion had continued to negotiate a settlement that would keep Luther from appearing before the diet—whether because he was working sincerely for the good of church and empire or because he was trying to arrange Luther's arrest, we cannot say with any certainty. The emperor had been ready to issue an edict against Luther. Luther himself harbored no illusions about the probable outcome at Worms. After the people of Erfurt welcomed him enthusiastically as he passed through their city, he remarked, "I have had my Palm Sunday" (a reference to Jesus' entry into Jerusalem on the Sunday before his crucifixion). On another occasion he said he would go to Worms even if there were as many devils there as tiles on the roofs. On April 16 Luther and a few companions rode into Worms in a cart accompanied by the imperial herald.

In the late afternoon of the next day the herald led Luther before the emperor, the electors, and representatives of the estates. The emperor, square-jawed and youthful, observed the middle-aged monk and remarked to those standing near him, "He will never make a heretic out of me." As Luther had suspected, there would be no debate. Shown a pile of his books, the emperor's representative asked if they were his. If Luther wished, this was his chance to disown his more controversial writings, especially the *Prelude on the Babylonian Captivity of the Church*. He owned them all and added that he had written even more than had been displayed. When asked if he wished to stand by all he had written or reject some of it, he asked for time to think about such an important matter. Reluctantly, the emperor gave him twenty-four hours. Why Luther asked for this delay is not clear. If he was hesitant to stand by all of his books in the afternoon, he had made up his mind to do just that by the evening. When Luther appeared for his audience the next day, other business kept him standing and waiting for two hours. Finally, at six o'clock, he stood before the emperor in the crowded hall to give his answer. Luther spoke at length about the different kinds of books he had written and the different issues he had raised. He admitted that in some he had been more violent than perhaps he should have been, adding, "But then, I do not set myself up as a saint; neither am I disputing about my life, but about the teaching of Christ." He asked again to be shown his error from Scripture: "I ask by the mercy of God, may your most serene majesty, most illustrious lordships, or anyone at all who is able, either high or low, bear witness, expose my errors, overthrow them by the writings of the prophets and evangelists." Luther, of course, still wanted a debate. The emperor's representative asked him for a clear and simple answer to the question rather than a "horned" response.

The full text of what Luther said next comes from an account of the diet composed either by someone friendly to Luther, perhaps with Luther's assistance, or by Luther himself. (The account that came from the papal party only summarizes Luther's replies. Both of these contemporary accounts are extremely one-sided.) To the request for a clear answer Luther replied:

> Since then your serene majesty and your lordships seek a simple answer, I will give it in this manner, neither horned nor toothed: Unless I am convinced by the testimony of Scriptures or by clear reason (for I do not trust either in the pope or in councils alone, since it is well known that they have often erred and contradicted themselves), I am bound by the Scriptures I have quoted and my conscience is captive to the Word of God. I cannot and I will not retract anything, since it is neither safe nor right to go against conscience. I cannot do otherwise, here I stand, may God help me. Amen.

With time running short, the imperial spokesman, according to the papal account, seized on Luther's mention of councils and conscience: "Lay aside your conscience, Martin; you must lay it aside because it is in error; and it will be safe and proper for you to recant. Although you say the councils have erred you will never be able to prove it." Shouting to be heard over the crowd, Luther said he could prove it. With that the diet recessed and guards swept Luther from the hall for his own safety. Other guards standing outside, part of the emperor's contingent from Spain, sneered at Luther, thinking that perhaps he was on his way to be burned at the stake.

Now the diet had to decide what to do with Luther. The emperor had made up his mind. The day after Luther's hearing Charles disseminated a declaration that affirmed his adherence to the Catholic faith of his ancestors and also affirmed his certainty that Luther, rather than the church, was in error. "For that reason," the emperor wrote, "I am absolutely determined to stake on this cause my kingdoms and seignories, my friends, my body and blood, my life and soul." Charles added that he would honor the safe conduct he had granted Luther but would also "proceed against him as a notorious heretic." He expected the princes to do the same.

On that same day a notice appeared in the city suggesting that the peasants would rise up in Luther's defense. Luther spent the next few days receiving guests who wished him well and debating with some of his opponents who did not. He appeared before a group of princes and archbishops who attempted to persuade him to submit to church and emperor. When Luther left the city ten days after he had arrived, the leaders of the Holy Roman Empire were still debating his fate. Elector Frederick of Saxony, Luther's prince, and another elector had refused to approve the emperor's judgment against Luther. On May 6, the emperor brought to the diet the draft of an edict against Luther that had been prepared by Jerome Aleander, the papal representative. But when Aleander presented the text of the edict to Charles for his signature, he refused to sign, saying that the assembly must approve it. Charles made the edict official twenty days later, asking the diet to approve it only after most of Luther's supporters had left Worms. The Edict of Worms called Luther "this devil in the habit of a monk" and added, "He lives the life of a beast." The Lutheran princes, who stood condemned along with Luther, objected that only a handful had been present to approve the Edict.

Luther at Wartburg Castle

Because the Imperial Edict gave Luther's enemies permission to apprehend him, his friends decided to kidnap him before anyone else could. On the way home to Wittenberg armed horsemen attacked Luther and his companions. Luther and one of the men had been warned this would happen, but the others watched helplessly as Luther was dragged from the wagon and taken away on horseback. After a day's ride Luther arrived at Wartburg Castle, high on a hill above the town of Eisenach. His disappearance fed rumors that he was dead. Soon word came that Luther lived but was hidden away, perhaps in Bohemia. Elector Frederick, who had ordered the abduction, was keeping Luther prisoner for his own safety. At the castle the professor laid aside the cowl he had worn for more than fifteen years as a monk to dress as a knight; he even let his beard grow as part of the disguise. The warden and servant boys in the castle called him "Knight George."

Luther might have looked the part of a knight but had little interest in the life of the castle. One day he joined a hunting expedition. The way the hounds chased rabbits horrified him, and Luther managed to save one. He rolled it up in his cloak and then set the cloak aside. The dogs found it and bit through the cloak to kill the rabbit. Luther saw the incident as an image of how the devil pursues Christians, perhaps because he felt that he was under attack physically and spiritually at the Wartburg. Insomnia and constipation plagued him. At night the strange noises of the castle sounded to him as if the devil were rolling casks in order to disturb his sleep. The responsibility he had shouldered by opposing the pope and the church tormented his conscience. He asked himself the question others had asked: How do you know that you are right when so many disagree? Then, convinced he was right, he berated himself for not having spoken even more boldly.

Despite these difficulties, Luther's time at the Wartburg was remarkably productive. At the castle he wrote some dozen treatises, numerous letters, and translated the New Testament into German. Books were his entertainment, and writing substituted for preaching to his congregation and talking with his friends and colleagues. In some treatises, he continued to defend his ideas against the attacks of his opponents. In others, he addressed the people of Wittenberg, guiding them from afar as they tried to reform the church in his absence. In place of preaching, which he normally did several times a week, Luther substituted work on his *Postills*, a collection of sermon studies for every Sunday of the year. Through this collection, Luther's thoughts and words eventually sounded forth from pulpits throughout Germany.

By far the most important work Luther undertook at the Wartburg was his translation of the Bible. All but alone in the castle, Luther had the time to implement a key piece of his plan for reform. Over the course of eleven weeks he produced a New Testament in German. It would be printed in September 1522, after Luther's return to Wittenberg and just in time for the Frankfurt book fair. With his New Testament translation selling briskly, Luther began to translate the Old Testament with the help of numerous colleagues. Because the Old Testament is much longer than the New and because the Hebrew text was difficult for the translation team, the entire Bible in German would not be ready for publication until 1534. Immensely popular at the time, the enduring significance of Luther's Bible lies in why and how he made his translation.

The reason Luther wanted a German Bible stems from his conviction that Scripture alone should be authoritative for Christian faith and life. Furthermore, Luther believed that all Christians, not just the clergy, should decide whether or not a teaching or practice conformed to Scripture. He thought the Bible was sufficiently clear that any Christian reading it could grasp its essential meaning. It only remained to provide a Bible that all Christians could read, or at least have read to them. For his German audience, Luther would produce a German translation of the Bible. The Latin text (or Vulgate—Jerome's translation of the Bible) had been authoritative throughout the Middle Ages. Because medieval theologians believed that the biblical text was often obscure and that its true meaning was to be found in spiritual senses of the text, the fact that Latin could be read and used only by educated specialists presented no problem. But some specialists disagreed. John Wyclif (d. 1384) is the most well known of those scholars who called for a vernacular Bible before Luther. His ideas spurred English translation work and gave rise to the anticlerical Lollard movement, which in turn brought the church's wrath upon English Bibles and those who used them. Luther, of course, faced similar opposition to his new translation—not because a German Bible was in itself controversial, but because he expected common people to use it.

Other German Bibles had been printed before Luther began his work. In fact, prior to 1500 more Bibles had been printed in German than in any other vernacular language. Luther's translation surpassed these earlier versions in two important ways. First, Luther strove for a meaningful rendering of the text. That meant beginning with the original Greek. In debate with his opponents, Luther had frequently appealed to the original Greek text of the New Testament where it differed from the Latin Vulgate translation. Now in his translation work he used the latest humanist scholarship—Erasmus's 1519 edition of the Greek New Testament. (He also consulted the Vulgate and other German translations as well.) Luther worked diligently to express the meaning of the Greek text in understandable German. Earlier German translations of the Bible had rendered the Latin of the Vulgate word for word, resulting in a wooden and grammatically obscure German. Luther intentionally worked at the level of meaning rather than words. Years later, he wrote about how difficult translation work was and how he worked through the biblical text "meaning by meaning" when he translated. The second way in which Luther's German Bible surpassed its predecessors is the kind of German the reformer employed. Luther worked to use a German that would be accessible to anyone who spoke the language. He avoided dialects, which in that day differed drastically from one another, and language specific to the upper class. His translation succeeded so well that it became the model for the common language that is modern German.

Excursus: Printing and the Reformation

As Luther intended, his translation of the Bible helped to spread the ideas of the Reformation. But the translation itself could be spread widely only through the technology of printing with moveable type. Protestant reformers took advantage of vernacular literacy, on the rise in the late Middle Ages, to take their ideas directly to the people through the power of the press. In the early years of the Reformation, Protestants published far more works than their Catholic opponents.

Printing with moveable type had been invented in Germany around 1440. Johann Gutenberg of Mainz brought together in a practical system the printing press, oil-based ink, and mass-produced metal type. Copies of his most famous work, a printed edition of the Bible in Latin, created a sensation at the diet of Frankfurt in October 1454. Noted humanist Enea Sylvia Piccolomini, who later became Pope Pius II, called Gutenberg "a remarkable man" and observed that his printed Bible could be read easily without spectacles. The technology spread so quickly that by 1500 many seemingly unimportant towns had their own presses.

Martin Luther took advantage of printers and they took advantage of him. As we have seen, the 95 Theses were translated from Latin into German and printed without Luther's authorization because the printers were convinced they would sell. The indulgence that provoked the theses had itself been printed in quantities sufficient to support sales. Copyright did not exist and authors were compensated for their work, if they were compensated at all, through patronage—sponsorship by a wealthy donor. Luther, nevertheless, willingly fed the presses in order to spread his ideas quickly and effectively. Many printers chose to print or not to print Luther's works out of conviction, but those who published volumes by Luther were never blind to the economic advantage they gained. Luther's books sold well. Two early Latin editions of his works (1518 and 1519) sold out completely. Four thousand copies—more than four times a normal run—of *To the Christian Nobility* were printed in August 1520. The treatise was printed again only five days later and went through fifteen more printings after that!

While he was at the Wartburg, Luther managed the printing of his works through correspondence with Georg Spalatin, his liaison to Elector Frederick. In these letters we see how he shepherded works through the press, giving priority to those works he thought most important. He also expressed frustration with the delay in printing some of his writings, asking in one letter, "For goodness' sake, is my *Magnificat* not yet finished?" When he returned to Wittenberg from the Wartburg, Luther immediately set about readying the German New Testament for the printers. At first several different printers published editions of the text. Eventually Luther restricted printing of the Bible to one Wittenberg firm in order to assure the quality of the text. He developed his seal—a rose with a heart and cross in the center—for the same reason. Quickly set editions of his works riddled with errors aggravated Luther. The presence of his rose on the title page of a work indicated that the reformer himself had authorized the text.

Luther in His Own Words

The selection presented here is the first portion of *On the Freedom of a Christian*. These paragraphs demonstrate how Luther used paradoxical statements to explain his theological insights and how he related those statements to the religious practices of his day.

First, so that we can know what a Christian is and what should be believed about the freedom (about which St. Paul wrote so much) that Christ won for and gave to the Christian, I will set forth these two conclusions:

A Christian is a free lord over all things and subject to no one.

A Christian is a subservient slave in all things and subject to everyone.

These two conclusions are clearly stated by St. Paul in 1 Corinthians 9, "I am free in all things and have made myself a slave to everyone." He also says in Romans 13, "You should owe no one anything, except that you love one another." But love is subservient and subject to the one who is loved. So also it says of Christ in Galatians 4, "God sent forth his son, born of a woman and made subservient to the law."

Second, we should think of these two opposing statements on freedom and subservience in this way: every Christian is of two natures, spiritual and bodily. According to the soul, the Christian is called a spiritual, new, and inner person. According to flesh and blood, the Christian is called a bodily, old, and outward person. And for the sake of this distinction between soul and body—these things that are so directly opposed to each other—that the Scriptures use to describe the Christian, I will now say the same thing about freedom and subservience.

Third, we take up the topic of the inner person, to see what belongs to that person who is and is called a pious, free Christian. It is clear that no outward thing makes the Christian free or pious because neither the Christian's piety and freedom, nor the Christian's wickedness and bondage, are bodily or outward. What does it help the soul if the body is at liberty, hale and hearty, and eats, drinks, and lives as it will? Again what does it harm the soul if the body is imprisoned, is sick and weak, thirsts and suffers as it does not wish to do? These things don't reach the soul even a bit to make it free or imprisoned, pious or impious.

Fourth, it also does nothing to help the soul that the body wears holy garments, as the priests and religious people [i.e., monks and nuns] do, or whether the body is in the church or in a holy place. Nor does it help the soul to process with holy relics, to pray, to fast, to go on pilgrimage, or to do all sorts of good works, even if such things could be done by the body eternally! It must always be otherwise—that the soul brings and gives piety and freedom. A person can have all the abovementioned items, works, and ways and still be an impious person, a fraud and a hypocrite. And through such conduct people become nothing more than idle frauds. Let me say it again—it does no harm to the soul if the body wears unholy clothes, is in an unholy place, neither eats, drinks, goes on pilgrimage, or prays, and leaves all works undone, as the aforementioned hypocrites do.

4

The Reformer (1522–1529)

Unrest in Wittenberg and Luther's Return

Neither the Edict of Worms nor Luther's seclusion at the Wartburg put a halt to attempts at church reform. Luther's absence did not even slow reform in Wittenberg, since his numerous colleagues carried on in his absence. Certain of the Augustinian monks, university professors, and leaders among the citizenry sought to change church practices in the city in order to bring them in line with Luther's ideas. Because they did not always agree among themselves on precisely how to effect reform, chaos constantly threatened to overtake their good intentions. Those who preferred the papal church resisted any change at all, and the elector himself, fearing anarchy, put a stop to proposed changes on several occasions.

Two significant issues occupied reformers and opponents of reform in Wittenberg—the question of monastic vows and the Mass. Gabriel Zwilling, the leader of reform within the Augustinian monastery, preached passionately against monasticism, and many monks left the monastery to marry and pursue other occupations. Even some who agreed that priests should be free to marry could not fathom the idea that monks should break their vows. Luther himself asked incredulously from his perch in the castle, "Good Lord! Will our people at Wittenberg give wives even to the monks? They will not push a wife on me!" Personal preference aside, Luther feared that some who left the monastery were not firmly convinced it was the right thing to do. He responded to the situation in the treatise *On Monastic Vows*. He argued that the church's understanding of monastic vows had contradicted his understanding of the gospel. Most monks believed that by taking their vows, they were performing a work that would help to save them. Such vows could be renounced with a clear conscience. But if a monk had understood his vows correctly, that is, not as contributing to his salvation, and taken them freely, he should keep them. In the end, Luther assured his fellow Augustinians who had left the Wittenberg monastery that the choice was theirs to make. Luther's approach to monastic vows underscores the concern for Christian conscience that would inform his response to even greater unrest in the near future.

That greater unrest came over reform of the Mass. Zwilling, Luther, Melanchthon, and Karlstadt agreed that private Masses should cease and that all should receive the wine as well as the bread when they communed. Private Masses presented the problem of the Mass as sacrifice. When a priest celebrated Mass by himself, it could only be seen as a good work being offered to God. That contradicted Luther's understanding that in the sacrament God was the one offering something, namely, forgiveness. But stopping private Masses affected lay piety in a way that arguing over monastic vows did not. Pious people in the Middle Ages relied on private Masses, especially those said on behalf of relatives who had died. The elector himself resisted this change and encouraged the leaders in the monastery and the university to wait. He reacted in the same way to the idea that all should receive both bread and wine in communion, contrary to the medieval practicing of giving only the bread. In September 1521, Melanchthon gathered in his home with some university students to celebrate Mass in both kinds (as receiving both bread and wine was commonly called). A month later the Augustinian monks began to receive both kinds. When the prior of the monastery forbade this practice, the monks stopped celebrating Mass entirely. The controversy escalated over when and how to introduce this change to the lay people of Wittenberg.

Just at that time, Luther visited the city in his disguise as Knight George. Concerned about reports he had heard, Luther arrived in Wittenberg early in December. His friends failed to recognize him at first. As something of a joke, they then asked Lucas Cranach to paint a portrait of the visiting knight. The Wittenberg artist produced yet another significant portrayal of Luther, this time with his knight's beard. After several days of conversation, Luther left for the Wartburg satisfied with the direction of the reform efforts in Wittenberg. This in spite of the fact that during his visit university students had harassed some priests celebrating Mass and, the next day, the Franciscan monks of the city. Either Luther did not know about these events or excused them as youthful excess. He did not condone violence as a means of reform. In fact, when he returned to the castle, he wrote a treatise titled *A Sincere Admonition to All Christians to Guard Against Insurrection and Rebellion*. In it he encouraged his followers to bring reform about through patient teaching rather than through revolution. He warned against a partisan spirit, reminding them that they were Christians and not Lutherans, that is, followers of Christ not of Luther. (He was not successful in his campaign against the name *Lutheran*.) Luther's counsel of reliance on careful instruction would be sorely needed in the months ahead.

Once Luther had returned to the Wartburg, new difficulties arose in Wittenberg. At the end of December Karlstadt led the Wittenberg congregation in celebrating an "evangelical" Mass, that is, one that conformed to the way the reformers read the Gospels. He did not wear the priestly vestments, spoke in German, and insisted that everyone present receive both bread and wine. The changes themselves reflected the spirit of Luther's reform, but the way they were carried out, through coercion rather than education, did not. Karlstadt's very public celebration of his marriage in January caused further controversy because as a priest and professor he would traditionally not have married.

In the same month, the "Zwickau prophets" appeared in the city. Nicholas Storch, a weaver, led the group from the Saxon town of Zwickau. Storch believed that the Holy Spirit inspired him directly and had called him to be a reformer. Because Storch thought the Holy Spirit worked directly, he did not believe the Bible to be entirely necessary and rejected all clergy as well as infant baptism. Zwickau had already experienced some conflict over reform ideas, and the town council was not inclined to take action against the small group of more radical reformers led by Storch. Finally, action by the government of Electoral Saxony forced Storch out of the city. Storch and two others made their way to Wittenberg. There they made a profound impression on Luther's colleagues, especially Melanchthon. Amidst the upheaval of reformation, it seemed to him quite plausible that men with the kind of gifts Storch claimed should arise in the church. It seemed far less plausible to Elector Frederick and to Luther. The elector simply instructed Melanchthon to refute the "prophets" from Scripture and send them on their way. Luther's letter to Melanchthon was equally blunt: "I do not approve of your timidity, since you are stronger in spirit and learning than I." Luther then went on to provide reasoned arguments against the "prophets." He recognized, however, that the question of the validity of infant baptism in particular would not be solved so easily. "I have always expected Satan to touch this sore," he wrote, "but he did not want to do it through the papists. It is among us and our followers that he is stirring up this grievous schism, but Christ will quickly trample him under our feet." The "Zwickau prophets" left Wittenberg, but, as Luther suspected, their ideas would crop up again to drive approaches to church reform more radical than his own.

A final instance of disorder surrounding the statues and paintings in the city churches prompted Luther to return several weeks earlier than planned. Karlstadt and Zwilling had both agitated for the removal of all images from the churches and preached sermons on the subject. A proposed church order for the city stipulated that images and side altars (altars along the sides of a church, usually dedicated to specific saints) should be removed. But citizens inflamed by the radical sermons of Karlstadt and Zwilling destroyed some of the images rather than simply allowing them to be taken down. Elector Frederick stepped in to restore order. Remaining images were left in place and Karlstadt and Zwilling would no longer be allowed to preach. The elector knew that this sort of anarchy only gave ammunition to the opponents of reform who were already planning to make their case at the next imperial diet. Luther, too, stepped in, deciding that he had to return to his Wittenberg pulpit. He had already planned to return at Easter but now left the Wartburg almost two months earlier and against the elector's wishes. Luther recognized that his return might cause further difficulties for Elector Frederick but decided that his continued absence would be worse. He wrote about the situation to the elector, punning on the ruler's fondness for collecting relics. "For many years Your Grace has been acquiring relics in every land," Luther wrote, "but God has now heard Your Grace's request and has sent Your Grace without cost or effort a whole cross, together with nails, spears, and scourges. I say again: grace and joy from God on the acquisition of a new relic!" Luther believed it a far greater thing to suffer because of the gospel than to sacrifice wealth to purchase relics. For himself, he was willing to live without the elector's promise of protection, believing that God was protecting him and promoting his cause.

Luther, still disguised as Knight George, left the Wartburg alone at the beginning of March 1522. When he stopped at a tavern along the way, he met two Swiss students who were on the way to Wittenberg. The students asked the knight whether Martin Luther was in Wittenberg, and the knight responded that he was expected soon. As they conversed, the knight emphasized how important Greek and Hebrew were for the study of theology. Then the students noticed that he was reading a Hebrew book of psalms! Luther encountered the students later at Wittenberg and enjoyed their surprise at discovering who their table companion at the tavern had been. Once in Wittenberg, Knight George again became Doctor Luther. Luther put on his monks' habit, cut his hair, and shaved his beard. On Invocavit Sunday, three days after his return and about six weeks before Easter, Luther looked down from his pulpit on the congregation at St. Mary's church. He preached the first of eight sermons—one each day until the next Sunday and later known as the "Invocavit Sermons"—addressing the reform of the church in Wittenberg. He chastised the citizens of Wittenberg and their leaders for the loveless way they had gone about reform. Luther had attacked the pope for commanding things that were not necessary for salvation and now he reprimanded the Wittenbergers for doing the same thing. They had forced people against their conscience to receive the sacrament in both kinds, among other changes. Luther promoted instead an agenda of patient instruction, rooted in the gospel and Christian freedom. His approach stood in contrast to Karlstadt's reforms that had forcefully and abruptly altered long-held practices. The sermons marked out a more stable path toward reform in Wittenberg, and Luther's return marked another stage in his evolution as a reformer.

Temporal Authority and the Spread of the Reformation

Wittenberg was the epicenter of the Reformation movement in the early 1520s. In addition to Luther himself, the university boasted other talented scholars who attracted students and promoted evangelical ideas. Philipp Melanchthon, the most prominent of Luther's colleagues, lectured to a packed hall and his *Loci Communes* became the premier textbook of theology. Luther was full of praise for Melanchthon. "That little Greek scholar outdoes me even in theology itself," he confided to a friend, and he enthusiastically recommended the *Loci Communes*. The activity of other Wittenberg colleagues also served to spread the Reformation. For example, Johannes Bugenhagen, who became pastor at the city church, where Luther had been doing much of the preaching, and also lectured at the university, helped to organize churches in territories throughout northern Europe.

Yet the University of Wittenberg and its scholars flourished only because Elector Frederick generally favored their efforts and successfully navigated the troubled waters of imperial politics. Reformers in other places were not always as fortunate. Duke Wilhelm of Bavaria, for example, legislated against Lutheran ideas at about the same time Luther returned to Wittenberg. Reformation ideas had already spread throughout Bavaria, and numerous groups defied the ban. The appearance of Luther's German Bible only added fuel to the fire. Among those pursued by the government for being Lutherans was a young theology student at Ingolstadt, Arsacius Seehofer. Seehofer had previously studied at Wittenberg, where he was influenced by Karlstadt and Melanchthon. Seehofer's arrest aroused protests that were quelled only by further arrests. A theological committee convicted Seehofer of seventeen "errors" drawn from the work of Melanchthon. The government offered him the reduced sentence of confinement in a monastery if he would recant. Seehofer, perhaps in light of the recent execution of two Lutherans in the Netherlands, placed his hand on the New Testament and tearfully recanted before the entire university of Ingolstadt.

One of those who had defended Seehofer was a remarkable Bavarian noblewoman, Argula von Grumbach. Her intervention in the Seehofer affair eloquently expresses the spread of Luther's ideas and the equalizing tendencies of the Reformation. Argula had studied the writings of Luther and his colleagues and read the Bible in light of them. Following Seehofer's conviction, she wrote to the University of Ingolstadt and to Duke Wilhelm, an old acquaintance. The opening salvo in her letter to the university refers to Seehofer's oath and sounds the Lutheran theme of the Word of God. "How in God's name can you and your university expect to prevail, when you deploy such foolish violence against the Word of God; when you force someone to hold the holy Gospel in their hands for the very purpose of denying it, as you did in the case of Arsacius Seehofer?" Argula defended her right to use Scripture and her own theological understanding in judging Seehofer's teaching. "In German not a single one [of Seehofer's statements that has been condemned] seems heretical to me. And the fact is that a great deal has been published in German, and I've read it all." Argula's own German Bible was a version that predated Luther's, and she expressed her confidence that what she read there would endure even if Luther himself defected from the cause of reform. "[I]f it came to pass—which God forfend—that Luther were to revoke his views, that would not worry me. I do not build on his, mine, or any person's understanding, but on the true rock, Christ himself." Argula's letter to Duke Wilhelm sounded a similar tone. Her theme was "the word of God alone should—and must—rule all things." For Argula *all things* included the rulers themselves, who should serve God's purpose. So it was appropriate that the title given the treatise when it was printed evoked Luther's *To the Christian Nobility*. Neither the University nor the Duke took kindly to Argula's intervention. As a result of her action, her husband lost his position. Nevertheless, Argula continued to work and write on behalf of the Reformation. She corresponded with Luther and even visited him when he remained behind at Coburg castle during the 1530 Diet of Augsburg.

Argula's experience in Bavaria shows how intertwined church and state were in the sixteenth century. Luther himself had called for the involvement of the nobles in the cause of church reform. When German rulers opposed reform and banned Luther's books and his Bible translation, he expressed more clearly his understanding of the relationship between church and government in the treatise *On Secular Authority*. First, he explained that rulers had a legitimate Christian calling as pleasing to God as any other. He argued against the medieval understanding that governing was somehow inherently sinful. He stated that rulers who used violence in punishing criminals and going to war did not violate the commands against murder because God had given them their vocation in order to serve others. Second, however, he cautioned rulers against overreaching. They did not rule over soul and conscience and could not coerce anyone to believe anything. For them to try was as foolish as it was for the bishops and other church leaders to claim temporal authority and power. Here he specifically mentions how books, including the German Bible, were being confiscated in territories like Bavaria. Finally, Luther concluded his treatise with advice to those who wished to be truly *Christian* rulers, admonishing them to rule justly and wisely. Luther still hoped that all rulers would follow Frederick's example and favor the Reformation and that those who did not would at least get out of the way. The treatise reflected the specific situation of the spread of reform in the early 1520s, but it also proved to be a touchstone for Luther's response to various crises of government, such as the peasant rebellions that were looming on the horizon as he wrote.

The Peasants' War

At this time in the history of the Holy Roman Empire, territorial princes were becoming more powerful at the expense of the emperor above them and the knights, townsmen, and peasants below them. The lower orders of society also felt themselves overburdened by rents, tithes, and taxes in the midst of a changing economy. These factors combined with the volatile religious situation to make the early 1520s a precarious time of revolt and rebellion.

The knights, under Franz von Sickingen, went to war in 1522. They attacked the Archbishopric of Trier, in part because of a feud between the archbishop and von Sickingen. But the Imperial Free Knights, that is, knights who owed allegiance to no lord but the emperor, had been dissatisfied and restless in the new political climate. With the increased use of mercenaries for warfare, their services on the battlefield were no longer needed, and the territorial princes were taking over many of the other sources of income the knights had relied on, such as collecting tolls on rivers. Although von Sickingen and others had hoped the new emperor would improve their lot, Charles offered little. The attack on Trier provided an occasion to mobilize the knights for greater activity in the reform of the empire. The princes, seeing an opportunity to eliminate the knights completely as a political power, came in force to aid the archbishop against them. The knights failed to take the city of Trier and dispersed to their individual castles. The princes hunted them down, using cannons to destroy the castle walls. Franz von Sickingen fell mortally wounded when his castle was besieged, and he died in May 1523. With von Sickingen's death the Knights' War was over and the age of the Imperial Free Knights came to an end.

Although von Sickingen himself, and other knights like Ulrich von Hutten, had supported reform and offered to put their forces at Luther's disposal, their war had been of little concern to Luther. When he heard about their uprising, he commented only that he thought it would have a bad end. Luther consistently rejected violence as a path to reform, and he feared anarchy. Both points are important for understanding his response to the series of peasant rebellions that shook the empire in 1524 and 1525.

During the spring and summer of 1524 some of the peasants in the Black Forest rebelled against their overlords. In one case, a countess's demand that the peasants leave off their harvest work to pick strawberries for her became the immediate cause of the revolt. Eventually the rebellious peasants formed together into large bands, attacking the palaces of nobles and bishops, as well as monasteries—abbots could be the most exacting landlords of all and, in any case, monastery storerooms were usually full. Some of these peasant armies even besieged cities and castles. As they marched, townsmen and miners often joined them in violently protesting their own unfair treatment at the hands of the rulers. The unrest spread northward and by spring of 1525 revolt wracked Luther's homeland of Thuringia, and his boyhood town of Mansfeld saw a rebellion of its miners. In Thuringia, Mühlhausen became the center of revolt and its leader was Thomas Müntzer, a former student of Luther's. Clergy led many of the peasant bands, and as might be expected, their leadership gave a distinctly religious over-tone to the peasants' demands. In Müntzer's case, this meant more than a call for the reform of the church. Müntzer believed that he was leading those chosen by God in an apocalyptic event that would place political power in the hands of the faithful and restore the apostolic church. Müntzer had preached similar ideas for years, first as pastor at Zwickau—a position obtained for him by Luther—then at Allstedt. His increasingly outspoken radicalism earned him both Luther's enmity and expulsion from Electoral Saxony. Müntzer went to Mühlhausen in 1524 and there formed the "Eternal League of God" to promote his goals. By May the fol-lowing year he was leading a peasant army toward the castle of the Count of Mansfeld. As his army sacked and looted castles and monasteries along the way, the combined forces of several princes, including the Count of Mansfeld, caught up with the peasants. The opposing forces met at Frankenhausen. Müntzer, knowing his army was dismayed at the sight of the princes' artillery ranged against them, promised his followers that he would magically catch the cannon-balls in his sleeves. In spite of his promise, the princes destroyed Müntzer's army. Müntzer himself fled the field but was captured and several weeks later tortured and executed at Mühlhausen. Other peasant armies met a similar fate, largely because they lacked cavalry and only rarely matched the princes in numbers of artillery pieces.

What made this series of rebellions and risings something that could be called a war, or even as one historian puts it "the revolution of the common man," were the ideas captured in a document called *The Twelve Articles* published in March 1525. The demands the articles made were mostly traditional—freedom from certain taxes, freedom to hunt, fish, and gather wood—but the first and last articles cast the peasants' cause as part of the Reformation. The first demanded the right to elect pastors in order to safeguard the preaching of the gospel, and the last sub-jected the demands made in the other articles to the judgment of Scripture. In other ways, too, the peasants appealed to Reformation ideas and to Luther him-self. Talk of replacing human law with the law of God animated many of the revolts. Luther's *Freedom of a Christian* and his understanding of the gospel were frequently cited as justification for the peasants' demands. Yet in the final analy-sis, the peasants' grievances differed little from those that had sparked previous rebellions. Nor did the peasants everywhere pursue their demands to the point of violence. In the Austrian Tyrol, where the Peasants' War found its last expression, Archduke Ferdinand, the emperor's brother, met demands similar to those of *The Twelve Articles* with negotiation and some concessions, and by doing so, he averted violent rebellion.

Luther himself responded very moderately to *The Twelve Articles*. He replied to them with his *Admonition to Peace,* unaware that violence had already broken out in the Black Forest. He cautioned the peasants not to overthrow the temporal order. But he also chided the rulers, telling them they had brought the situation on themselves by their injustice. Luther feared that if they continued to repress the gospel, the result would be further rebellion. As for most of the demands made by the peasants, sympathetic though he was to some of them, such matters concerned him little. He admonished both parties, "Now, dear sirs, there is nothing Christian on either side and nothing Christian is at issue between you; both lords and peasants are discussing questions of justice and injustice in heathen, or worldly, terms." He became much more concerned when violence broke out and his name was used to justify it. Less than a month after he wrote the *Admonition to Peace* he added a section to the treatise's third edition entitled *Against the Raging Peasants*. (This section was also published separately under the title *Against the Robbing and Murdering Hordes of Peasants*.) He accused the peasants of betraying the ideals expressed in their *Twelve Articles*. Now their violence and murder deserved death and damnation. Not only had they resorted to violence but even worse "they cloak this terrible and horrible sin with the gospel and call themselves 'Christian brethren.'" He urged the rulers to protect those suffering at the hands of the peasants. "Have mercy on these poor people! Let whoever can stab, smite, slay. If you die in doing it, good for you! A more blessed death can never be yours."

The princes did not need Luther's permission to suppress the peasants with overwhelming force, and brutal reprisals followed their defeat. The rebellious bands reaped a hundredfold the violence they had sown. Many who had participated in or were sympathetic to the rebellions felt Luther had betrayed them. Others, seeing the excesses committed by the princes against the peasants, criticized Luther for encouraging them to violence. He was called a "toady to the sovereigns"—a criticism that is often repeated today. Luther had an answer for those who found his response harsh and violent in his *Open Letter on the Harsh Book Against the Peasants*. "I reply, 'That is right.' A rebel is not worth rational arguments, for he does not accept them. You have to answer people like that with a fist. . . . He who will not hear God's word when it is spoken with kindness, must listen to the headsman, when he comes with his axe." Here Luther's blunt language obscured his principle. In *On Secular Authority* he had already expressed his conviction that the gospel could not be used to rule, since that was not its purpose. The kind of people who need rules and laws need to be kept in line by those bearing the sword, and God had established the authorities for that purpose. He was under no illusion about the goodness of those who governed, but he also thought people got the kind of government they deserved. The bottom line for Luther was that only passive resistance was appropriate when the

Photo 4-1   Martin and Katherine Luther as they appeared in 1529. Attributed to Lucas Cranach. Source: Art Resource/Bildarchiv Preussischer Kulturbesitz.

government was in the wrong. The peasants, he thought, should have suffered temporal privation as good Christians rather than resorting to violence. Whether or not one agrees with Luther, he was at least consistent. He would give the same answer to the Lutheran princes when the emperor threatened them with war.

Marriage

Luther's boast "They will not push a wife on me!" proved untrue in June of 1525. As the Peasants' War raged, he wrote to a friend, "If I can manage it, before I die I will still marry my Kate to spite the devil, should I hear that the peasants continue." "My Kate" was Katherine von Bora, the twenty-six-year-old daughter of an impoverished nobleman, who had gone to the convent as a child after her mother died. She was one of nine nuns who had fled their convent and come to Wittenberg in April 1523. Some eventually returned to their families, but others, like Katherine, no longer had family. These Luther tried to find a place for or, if they wished, a husband. Although Katherine was willing to marry, she had very specific ideas about whom she would marry. When Luther had proposed a match she considered unsuitable, she appealed to his university colleague Nicholas von Amsdorf. Katherine told von Amsdorf she would marry only him or Martin Luther.

At first, Luther had no wish to marry Katherine. He expected to be killed by the peasants or the emperor at any moment, and marriage was the farthest thing from his mind. Then Argula von Grumbach and other friends encouraged him to marry. They argued that it would strengthen the opponents of clergy marriage if Luther himself remained single. Katherine von Bora and Martin Luther married on June 13, 1525. It was a Tuesday—the customary day for weddings. Nicholas von Amsdorf would remain a lifelong bachelor. Katherine came to live with Martin in the Black Cloister, the Augustinian monastery in Wittenberg. Several years later, the elector gave the cloister to the Luthers as their home. Almost a year to the day after their wedding, Katherine and Martin had a son, Johannes, called Hans. Lucas Cranach stood as his godfather, as Luther did for Cranach's daughter Anna.

Marriage and a family changed Luther. It did not necessarily calm him down, as Melanchthon had hoped, but it did give him an even greater appreciation for ordinary, everyday life. He delighted to see things through the eyes of his children and took devious pleasure in verbal sparring with Kate. She grew into the role of manager of the Luther household, which normally included students and other guests. Although theirs had been an arranged marriage, as most were at that time, Katherine and Martin grew genuinely to love each other. When they were first married, Martin confessed his amazement at seeing pigtails on the pillow, but he soon became accustomed to the sight.

The Bondage of the Will

Luther finished *The Bondage of the Will,* which he later said was his best book, in December 1525. In it, he asserted more clearly than ever his belief that human beings relied entirely on God's grace for salvation. The human will was completely bound, as the title suggests, by sin and unable to make any move toward God. Salvation was accomplished, therefore, not by any human choice but by God's choice and by God's gift.

The Bondage of the Will responded point by point to a book by Erasmus that had appeared more than a year earlier, *The Free Will.* Erasmus had been pressured by his friends, and by some not-so-friendly forces, to distance himself from Luther. Erasmus chose the topic of the human will for this purpose because he found Luther's statements on the will to run counter to the tradition of the church, and because other possible topics, such as the power of the pope, would be a minefield. In *The Free Will,* Erasmus argued from Scripture, as Luther would require, with the help of the church fathers in interpreting the biblical texts. He presented the passages from the Bible that he thought spoke to both sides of the question of whether or not humans have free will in matters of salvation. He concluded there were enough clear passages on both sides of the question that Luther was wrong to assert that humans could not make any sort of free choice toward God. But he had also said he would prefer not to make any dogmatic assertions.

That statement was one of the many openings Luther exploited. He argued that without assertions there would be nothing to believe and charged Erasmus with gross impiety. "The Holy Spirit is no Sceptic!" he thundered. He meant that the biblical texts, believed to be the work of God the Holy speaking through human authors, spoke clearly about precisely the assertions Erasmus wished to avoid making. Luther had at first complained that Erasmus's work was not passionate enough to provoke a reply, but he gradually warmed to the topic. He credited Erasmus with choosing a topic that got to the heart of understanding the gospel. Then he proceeded to demolish Erasmus's method as well as his arguments. Luther found fault with the fact that the humanist resorted to statements from the church fathers to make his points rather than relying on Scripture alone. Luther asserted that the message of Scripture was clear and did not require the explanation of intermediaries. He continued, however, to state that even though Scripture was easy to understand, God was not. Erasmus had assumed in his explanations that God worked according to human standards of fairness and justice. It would be unjust for God to condemn those who could not also choose to believe. For Luther, this destroyed human reliance on God's grace and diminished God's power, since God should not be judged by what mere human beings might think just or fair. To explain his thought, he introduced the distinction between "God preached" and "God not preached." Clear biblical statements concerning God and salvation came under the heading "God preached." Trying to understand completely the God behind those statements, that is, trying to fill in any gaps with human reason, ventured into the territory of "God not preached." For Luther, some statements simply had to be held in tension rather than resolved. The same Scriptures that said God chooses those he will save also said God wants all people to be saved. Luther firmly believed that whatever appeared to human reason to be unjust in God would be revealed to be just and good in eternal life.

Erasmus responded with a work in two parts—each volume far longer than Luther's book. Luther made no further direct reply, although he continued to oppose Erasmus's position. The debate between them had two important consequences. First, humanists had to decide between Erasmus and Luther. Up to this point, men concerned with good letters, education, and reform had been able to claim both the Wittenberg professor and the great humanist author as one of them. Now the rift that had been growing for years had become clear and unavoidable, and humanists would fall out on both sides—some with the Protestant reformers and some remaining in the Roman church. Second, the topic of human will in salvation became a centerpiece in the Reformation debates, not just between Lutherans and Catholics but eventually between the followers of Luther and the followers of John Calvin. In *The Bondage of the Will*, in order to counter Erasmus's ideas of fairness, Luther had entertained the thought that the "God not preached" might choose people to be condemned as well as to be saved. But John Calvin, and especially his followers, would make that idea, known as double predestination, programmatic and eventually central to their theology. So Luther's heirs would have to fight the battle over human will on a brand-new front.

Reforming the Church in Saxony

When Luther returned to Wittenberg from the Wartburg, he felt the need to slow the pace of reform both because of what he considered Karlstadt's excesses and coercion and because of Elector Frederick's conservatism. When Frederick died in

May 1525, his brother John succeeded him. John supported changes to church practices and structures that would reinforce Luther's theology, and the church in Saxony was truly reformed during his reign.

At Christmas 1525, Luther's *German Mass* debuted in the Wittenberg church. Up until that point Wittenberg had used a slightly revised Latin Mass with an emphasis on the sermon and the reception of communion. In this new order of worship, German chorales sung by the congregation replaced the Latin chants performed by the choir. Luther intended that everything in the worship should serve to proclaim the gospel and teach the people. By the following spring, Elector John had mandated that the *German Mass* be used throughout Saxony. Luther, for his part, continued to write sermons and compose hymns for use throughout the territory and beyond. The musically gifted reformer was a competent composer, and many of his hymns are still sung today, particularly "A Mighty Fortress Is Our God." Luther had initially been reluctant to write an order of worship, fearing that his work would stifle the creativity of others. He did not believe any one single form of worship to be correct but asked only that whatever order was adopted support the gospel. He recognized that what Saxony, and even Wittenberg, still needed was patient and simple teaching.

That belief was reinforced when Elector John authorized a visitation of the churches in Saxony. Visitations had previously been conducted by the bishops and consisted of an investigation into the affairs of individual churches. The chaotic state of church finances provided the impetus for the visitations. People throughout Saxony had exercised their Christian freedom by refusing any longer to pay the tithe, a tax collected by the priests. As a result, preachers and teachers throughout the territory had almost no means of support. Luther and others had consistently urged the elector to restructure the finances of the churches in his territory. For that reason, teams that included government officials as well as theologians would conduct the visitations.

The visitations began in 1527. Melanchthon wrote instructions for the visitors to guide them in the doctrinal side of the visitations, and these were published in March 1528. Opponents of the Reformation ridiculed these instructions, not least as a return to the former way of doing things. One of Luther's old enemies created a caricature of a seven-headed Luther in which one head was labeled *visitor*. The doctrinal content of the instructions had caused some dissension even among Luther's followers. Nevertheless, the visitations proceeded. Luther served as part of a team for the area around Wittenberg. What he saw in his visits did not necessarily surprise him, but it did not please him either. Many parishes were poor, and in many more the parishioners neglected prayers and services. The preachers, many of them formerly Roman priests, could not preach properly—either out of ignorance or laziness, according to Luther.

He responded with two works on the catechism, that is, basic Christian texts like the Ten Commandments, the Apostles' Creed, and the Lord's Prayer. Luther used sermons he had preached in Wittenberg as the basis for *The Large Catechism*. He intended this work primarily for preachers to use in teaching their congregations. *The Small Catechism* was a very brief work meant for the instruction of lay people and use in the family. Luther intended it to be memorized easily, and it was first published in the form of placards to be hung on the wall. Both catechisms were published in 1529. The explanations in the catechisms expressed Luther's understanding of the essential aspects of the Christian faith and served also to form a distinctly Lutheran piety. Luther said that he himself remained a student of the catechism, returning to these essential texts as the foundation for his life as a Christian.

The catechisms also express Luther's focus on education at all levels, basic as well as advanced. We have already seen how Luther's reforming activity embraced and in many ways flowed out of the reform of the University of Wittenberg, which included the introduction of humanist subjects and method. In his preface to *The Small Catechism* he laid out an agenda for teaching the faith that progressed from learning the texts to learning their meaning and then to the material in *The Large Catechism*. University reform and catechisms both served the reform of the church. But Luther also promoted education for the betterment of society. Even *The Small Catechism* could be used in this way, according to its Preface. "Although no one can or should force another person to believe," he wrote, "nevertheless one should insist upon and hold the masses to this: that they know what is right and wrong among those with whom they wish to reside, eat, and earn a living." Five years earlier, Luther had articulated similar thoughts in his treatise *To the Councilmen of All the Cities in Germany That They Establish and Maintain Christian Schools*. The essential idea is laid out in the title: the cities should sponsor schools for all children—and here Luther, contrary to prevailing notions, included girls—to support the reform of the church, of course, but also to provide educated leaders for society. Luther and Lutherans who came after him remained ardent proponents of education at all levels.

The Marburg Colloquy

In September 1529 Luther, Melanchthon, and several colleagues traveled to Marburg, in the territory of Hesse, to meet with theologians from Zurich and southwest Germany. The meeting had been arranged by Philip of Hesse, one of the Lutheran princes, as an attempt to reach a theological agreement between the Zurichers and the Wittenbergers. But Philip was not necessarily interested in theology for its own sake. Those rulers who embraced the Reformation felt the need for a defensive alliance against their Catholic opponents, including the emperor. The rulers had been unable to forge a political alliance, however, because of doctrinal disagreements between their theologians. Like the emperor, the Lutheran princes believed that they could act in full concert only with others who shared their faith. Now Philip of Hesse had gathered the principal theologians together in an attempt to make a wider alliance possible.

Theologians representing the cities of Zurich, Basel, and Strasbourg met Luther and the others at Marburg. Of these, Huldrych Zwingli, the reformer of Zurich, was the most prominent. Zwingli, who was the same age as Luther, was a Roman Catholic priest who had come to the Reformation through humanism. He admired Erasmus deeply and pored over the New Testament in Greek. Although he read Luther, he admitted no influence from Luther on his own theology. In 1519

Zwingli had become the preacher in Zurich. He won the citizens of Zurich for the Reformation first through his preaching and then in 1523 through public debates against representatives of the Roman church. Like Luther he rejected the idea that works contributed to a person's salvation, but his understanding of faith had more of a communal focus than did Luther's. Zwingli retained the practice of baptizing infants over against some local critics only because he saw baptism as the means of entering the community. That same emphasis on community led him to reform not just the church but also the city, and he took an active role in civic affairs. Unlike Luther, he was not reluctant to bear arms, and he appeared at Marburg wearing a sword.

For several years prior to their meeting at Marburg, Luther and Zwingli were aware that they had parted ways on some significant points, most prominently over the Lord's Supper. Both reformers agreed that the meal Christ had instituted was not a sacrifice as the Roman church maintained. But Zwingli and Luther disagreed over what it was. According to the Gospel accounts of the Last Supper, Jesus said to his disciples, "This is my body" when he gave them bread and "This is my blood" when he gave them the cup of wine. This was the foundation of the sacrament. Luther took the words literally, believing that in some incomprehensible way the bread and wine were the body and blood of Christ. Christians ate them in a spiritual manner for the forgiveness of sins. Zwingli refused to accept the notion that God would ask anyone to believe against reason that the bread and wine were really and truly Christ's body and blood. He appealed to Bible passages such as "The Spirit gives life, the flesh counts for nothing" (John 6:63) to support his understanding. For Zwingli the meal was a commemorative event, and when Christians called to mind Christ's sacrificial death in this manner, he was spiritually present among them. Luther and Zwingli had debated each other in print for several years before meeting face-to-face.

On the first day of conversation at Marburg, Luther and Zwingli were purposely kept apart. The next day, October 2, at 6 o'clock in the morning, all the colloquy participants assembled for the conversation that would pit Luther and Melanchthon against Zwingli and his associate, Johannes Oecolampadius. Luther began by restating his position that he could find no scriptural basis for anything but a literal understanding of the words *This is my body*. Zwingli and Oecolampadius restated their position, noting that they and Luther agreed that the spiritual eating was the chief thing in the sacrament. Luther countered that Christ had also commanded a bodily eating. Though Zwingli could cite church fathers for his argument, Luther refused to give up the literal meaning of the words. When the debate began, he had written *Hoc est corpus meum* ("This is my body" in Latin) with chalk on the table where he was sitting and covered it with a cloth. Later on in the debate, Luther lifted up the cloth to reveal the words and said: "This is our Scripture passage. You have not yet taken it from us as you promised to do. 'This is my body.' I cannot pass over the text of my Lord Jesus Christ, but I must confess and believe that the body of Christ is there." Two days of discussion failed to bring about an agreement on this point, and the colloquy was brought to a conclusion because of an outbreak of fever. Philip of Hesse asked Luther to draft a set of articles outlining where the participants in the colloquy agreed and disagreed. Remarkably they were in agreement on fourteen out of fifteen articles—only the nature of the Lord's Supper stood between them.

When Luther returned to Wittenberg, he suffered once again from his bouts with despair (*Anfechtungen*). At Marburg he saw how divided the Reformation movement had become and how rulers and people continued to oppose the Word of God. The failure to find a political solution through the colloquy bothered him little. Luther had never seen the need for a defensive alliance. He believed that true Christians should suffer willingly for their faith. That belief would be put to the test in the months ahead as the emperor prepared to act against the Lutherans.

Writing History: The German Peasants' War

Historians vehemently disagree in their interpretation of Luther's response to the German Peasants' War. Many agree with the contemporary assessment that in this case Luther acted as a "toady to the princes," encouraging them against the peasants out of self-interest. Others would argue that, as frequently happened, his vehement language tended to obscure a legitimate and well-founded theological position. Differing ideas about the causes, goals, and effects of the war itself further complicate efforts to interpret Luther's response to the conflict. Events like the German Peasants' War can still arouse heated debate precisely because historical judgment cannot ultimately be separated from the historian's attitudes toward government and understanding of appropriate mechanisms for political change. So almost two centuries of historical interpretation has resulted in three major views: the Marxist, the political, and the sociological.

Friedrich Engels, the colleague of Karl Marx, inaugurated the Marxist approach with his 1850 work *The Peasant War in Germany*. For Engels, and Marxist historians after him, the war was an "early bourgeois revolution." This revolution marked a high point of class conflict that had begun with the Hussite wars of the fifteenth century. Luther inaugurated a first stage of the conflict in concert with the bourgeois capitalist class, but in the years following the Diet of Worms his moderate followers separated from more radical reformers and from the revolutionary peasants. Thomas Müntzer emerges from Engels's treatment as the hero because his teachings expressed the communist notions desired by the lower classes of society. Luther's ultimate approach to the peasants, on the other hand, betrayed the revolutionary proletariat, and the bourgeoisie and princes that he supported became the victors in the conflict. For Engels, this foreshadowed the betrayal of European revolutionaries in his own day: "Those classes and fractions of classes which everywhere betrayed 1848 and 1849, can be found in the role of traitors as early as 1525, though on a lower level of development." Since Engels, many historians, particularly those in the former East Germany, have expanded the Marxist interpretation.

The political approach to the German Peasants' War directly contradicts the Marxist understanding. First advanced by Gunther Franz in 1933, the political approach downplays class and economic factors. The peasants were not revolutionaries but reactionaries who wanted a return to an older form of justice and government. They were willing to adhere to the former understanding of service to their lords in return for protection. Their complaint was that the lords failed to protect them and had come to see the service of the peasants as a right that entailed no responsibility. The influential interpretation advanced by Peter Blickle sounds a variation on the political theme. The revolution did not belong to the peasants alone but to "the common man." Other groups, like citizens of the towns and cities, played a significant role in forming the political aims of the revolution, and it was the preachers who formed a link between them and the peasants in the common, and revolutionary, appeal to godly law coupled with the gospel. Although Blickle gives economic grievances their due as an initial cause, the revolution moved beyond them into the political sphere as the "common man" challenged the preeminence of the princes.

Sociological approaches to the German Peasants' War look to economic and concomitant social changes as the primary cause of the conflict. At first glance, this approach might seem similar to the Marxist understanding. But rather than focusing on the bourgeoisie and capitalism like the Marxists, historians adopting the sociological approach focus on the agrarian economy. Changes to that economy, some that enhanced the wealth and position of many peasants and some that brought increased hardship to many others, emerge as the single most important factor driving the peasants' actions. Historians who adopt the sociological approach agree with the political approach in identifying the overthrow or at least revision of the feudal contract as the goal of the peasant movement. Their activity was not, however, ideologically driven, as the political understanding would have it. The peasants rebelled out of hardship and frustration with their condition.

So Luther may have been responding to a simple rebellion, a proletarian revolution, an attempted return to old law, a "revolution of the common man," or economic protest on a massive scale, and he fares better in some historical accounts than in others. Engels casts him as a traitor to the cause; the sociological approach marginalizes Luther because he dealt in ideas rather than economic reality; the political approach sees an ideological division between Luther and the revolution. In the end, whether or not one believes Luther should have been more sympathetic to the peasants' cause will depend on what one believes about that cause.

5

The Preacher (1530–1546)

Introduction

"We are beggars. This is true." The last words Luther wrote reflect his reliance on God's grace. Luther had attempted throughout his career to communicate his belief that God was gracious through his writing and preaching. So these final words are appropriate for a chapter in which the theme is Luther the preacher. Luther was a preacher not only in the sense that he continued to preach in Wittenberg but in the broader sense that he had become *the* preacher, that is, the theological authority for his followers. In these years we find Luther affirming, defending, and disseminating the discoveries he had made in the previous decades.

By this time, however, many other reformers with other ideas about reformation were active throughout Europe. Luther was in many places no longer the most prominent Protestant reformer. Although he remained influential, the story of his life from about 1530 on is not as closely bound up with the history of the Reformation in a general sense as his life up to that point had been. Other leaders, especially John Calvin in Geneva, emerged to both build on and depart from what Luther had begun.

For their part, Luther and his followers had to defend their teaching before the emperor in the context of his wars against France and the Turks. They did this in a series of diets culminating at Augsburg in 1530. Although the emperor rejected the Lutheran confession of faith, negotiations after the diet led to a religious truce. Luther tried not to involve himself in imperial politics afterward but confined himself to theology, and the story of his life after this point can be told with little recourse to the political. Yet he continued vigorously to promote his cause, whether through lectures to his students or in many and varied treatises against those he considered his opponents. In these controversies, the unattractive aspects of Luther's personality are displayed prominently, but from his viewpoint the polemic was so bitter only because the issues were so important. When Luther died, he left as his legacy a movement that had divided but also reinvigorated the church and ideas—about theology, language, and education to name a few areas of his influence—that would bear fruit for generations to come.

Attempts to Enforce the Edict of Worms

During the 1520s Emperor Charles V, although opposed to Luther's teachings, had been unable to move successfully against Luther and the princes who supported him. War against France preoccupied the emperor for much of that time, and the Turks continually threatened the borders of the empire. To fight the French and repel the Turks, Charles needed the support of the German rulers and could not afford to antagonize them by dealing too highhandedly with the evangelical princes. Even many princes who remained firmly in the Roman Catholic fold were reluctant to see the emperor consolidate his power through a triumph against their Lutheran peers. Further complicating matters, Charles himself was not present for the negotiations about the religious situation within the empire but had deputized Archduke Ferdinand, his brother, to act on his behalf.

The 1521 Edict of Worms complicated the religious question rather than resolving it. The evangelical princes ignored the edict, and the pope's representatives bridled at Charles V's presumption in judging Luther after he had been excommunicated. A conflict over religion seemed imminent. During the uneasy years following the Diet of Worms, alliances and rumors of alliances became the order of the day. After the 1524 Diet of Nuremberg, at which the princes promised to observe the edict of Worms only as far as possible—which for many of them meant not at all, some of the Catholic rulers formed an alliance led by Archduke Ferdinand. The evangelical princes responded with their own negotiations toward a defensive alliance. Luther responded to the princes as he had to the peasants. They could defend themselves if attacked by an equal, but to go to war against the emperor, even in a just cause, would be rebellion. Yet by 1528 the mere rumor of another Catholic alliance led Philip of Hesse to go beyond the idea of a defensive alliance and argue for a preemptive war against the Catholic opponents. When he tried to convince Elector John of Saxony to join him, Luther argued forcefully against the plan, threatening to leave Electoral Saxony if John participated in such an enterprise. Luther persuaded the elector to shun Philip's scheme.

War against France

As the evangelical princes began to plan strategy, the emperor planned a war against France. He would launch invasions from England and the empire coupled with a rebellion by the Constable of France against King Francis I. Even though the scheme failed, the pope was sufficiently agitated that he allied himself with France to restore a balance of power, further straining his relationship with Charles. While the German Peasants' War was reaching its height, imperial forces defeated the French at the battle of Pavia and captured King Francis. He regained his freedom after signing a treaty, which he repudiated once safely back in France. The war with France continued as the imperial estates met at the (first) Diet of Speyer in the summer of 1526. On August 27, they agreed that each region should proceed as it saw fit in matters of religion, at least until a general council could meet. The emperor, because of the pope's alliance with France, neither endorsed nor opposed this solution. Two days after the diet reached its verdict, the Turks defeated a Hungarian army at Mohács and killed King Louis II. Louis had been linked by marriage to Ferdinand, Charles V's brother, who upon Louis's death inherited his crown and with it a primary role in the struggle against the Turks.

Meanwhile, imperial troops continued their campaign against the French in northern Italy. The armies of both sides consisted mostly of mercenaries who fought for pay and looted when they were not paid, which happened more often than not. In May 1527 an imperial army whose pay was several months in arrears sacked their way to the walls of Rome itself. On May 6 they took the city and made their way to St. Peter's Basilica, where they massacred the Swiss guards defending the pope. Pope Clement VII escaped to the Castel Sant'Angelo but with imperial troops marauding through the streets, he remained a virtual prisoner there. After a month's confinement the pope surrendered and paid a ransom to the emperor. Clement would no longer openly oppose Charles V. (Up to this point, in fact, the popes had refused to bestow the imperial crown on Charles. Clement would finally crown him in February 1530.) The emperor, although he denied responsibility for the attack, did not repudiate the results of the sack. Luther, in a letter to a friend, commented, "Rome and the pope have been terribly laid waste. Christ reigns in such a way that the emperor who persecutes Luther for the pope is forced to destroy the pope for Luther." Following the sack of Rome, the famed Venetian admiral Andrea Doria entered imperial service. With his fleet commanding the Mediterranean, Francis I had little choice but to come to terms with Charles. The two monarchs signed the Peace of Cambrai in August 1529.

The Turks Attack Vienna

As the ink dried on the peace treaty between France and the empire, an Ottoman Turkish army was marching toward Vienna. Sultan Suleiman's troops had set out from Bulgaria in the spring, slogging through the mud on their way to conquer Hungary. The city of Buda fell to the Turks early in September, and by the end of the month Suleiman's army reached Vienna. When the city declined to surrender, the Turkish artillery began a bombardment. The artillery could do little damage, however, because the sultan's largest guns had been left behind months before hopelessly stuck in the mud. The Turks next attempted to undermine the city walls. When this tactic, too, proved unsuccessful, they launched a final assault on October 14, but the city defenders drove them away. The Sultan's troops began to break camp that evening, and the siege was over. Luther was convinced that divine intervention had saved the empire from the Turks. He relayed news that the siege had been lifted to his colleague Nicholas von Amsdorf, concluding, "God has obviously fought for us this year." Luther also asked von Amsdorf to pray, which was his advice to all Christians in order to combat the Turkish threat. He urged those given the task of defending the people with armed force, such as the emperor, to do so to the best of their ability. At the same time, Luther believed God was using the threatening Turkish armies to bring the Germans to repentance, and for that reason prayer was ultimately the best weapon. Luther was convinced that the end of the world was near and saw the Turks as perhaps fulfilling the prophecies about the last days found in biblical books like Daniel and Ezekiel. During 1529 he commented frequently on these prophecies and even shifted his Old Testament translation work to the book of Daniel.

The Diet of Augsburg

The Turkish defeat at Vienna allowed the emperor, who at the same time had been temporarily freed from conflict with France, to turn his attention to the Lutherans at the Diet of Augsburg in 1530. The imperial estates had met at Speyer for a second time in spring 1529. At this diet Archduke Ferdinand condemned the idea resulting from the first Diet of Speyer that each ruler had the right to reform the church in his territory. In addition, he demanded that traditional Catholic practice should be tolerated everywhere. The princes and representatives of cities who opposed these demands lodged a formal protest and as a result became known as *Protestants*. So when Charles returned to Germany to preside at his first diet since Worms, he faced not just a single heretic in the person of Martin Luther but a confederation of territories that had embraced Luther's ideas. Personally, Charles was no more tolerant of what he termed heresy than he had been nine years earlier, but he also desired unity within the empire in order to face the constant threat from the Ottoman Turks. For that reason, he even considered making concessions in the sphere of religion.

Elector John would not permit Luther to attend the Diet of Augsburg because the city was outside Electoral Saxony, where he was relatively safe despite his status as an outlaw. If Luther could not go to Augsburg, he would have preferred to stay in Wittenberg, but the elector had other plans. Luther was to stay in the city of Coburg—close to Augsburg but still in the elector's territory—and be available for consultation. Philipp Melanchthon would be the principal theologian of their delegation to the diet. Those who would travel to Augsburg and those who would stay behind with Luther in Coburg gathered in that city in April. No one knew what to expect from the emperor, and the mood of the group vacillated between hope and fear. Luther could not guarantee the emperor's favor but reminded them all of his firm conviction that their cause was God's cause. On the Saturday before Easter, he preached to the assembled group, explaining that at such a time Christians might have to suffer for the sake of the gospel just as Christ himself suffered. Luther used the legend of St. Christopher as an illustration of this.

Christopher had agreed to carry a small child across a river. When he got out into the water, he found the child so heavy that he almost drowned. On reaching the other side, he learned that he had carried the Christ child and had truly had the weight of the world on his shoulders. Large paintings of St. Christopher were common in churches at this time and everyone knew the story well. Luther told his audience that they were like Christopher—carrying Christ in the world and suffering under the burden. He admitted "there is such threatening and terror that we would be frightened to death if we did not have another consolation to oppose it." For Luther the consolation was far greater than the threats because it was God's promise of salvation. With this encouragement, the Electoral Saxon delegation set out a week later for Augsburg. Luther moved into the elector's castle at Coburg. While he waited for the baggage containing his books and papers to catch up with him, he wrote letters to his friends who had gone on to the diet. In one, he compared the crows gathering outside the castle windows to the participants in that meeting. "Here [among the crows] you might see magnanimous kings, dukes, and other noblemen of the kingdom, who seriously care for their belongings and offspring, and who with untiring voice proclaim their decisions and dogma through the air." This humorous approach to the diet might seem an odd contrast to Luther's sermon, but both express his conviction that the situation was ultimately in God's hands.

That conviction would, however, be tested as Luther waited anxiously for word from Augsburg. He wrote frequently to his friends there, but they were too busy or too preoccupied to respond immediately, and he complained bitterly when no one wrote back to him with news. For more than a month, there was little to report, since the emperor did not arrive in Augsburg until June 15. Meanwhile, Luther kept busy writing (among other things, an exhortation to the bishops gathering at Augsburg to reform the church), translating (more of the Old Testament as well as Aesop's fables), and receiving visitors. In a letter to his wife, Kate, at the beginning of June, he reported that Argula von Grumbach had visited Coburg castle, and he passed along her advice for weaning little Magdalena Luther. The topic came up because Kate had sent Martin a drawing of Magdalena, which he promptly displayed in his room at the castle. At the same time, Luther received the news that his father, Hans, had died. "This death has certainly thrown me into sadness." Martin wrote, "The pity of heart and the memory of the most loving dealings with him have shaken me in the innermost parts of my being, so that seldom if ever have I despised death as much as I do now." Yet Luther also continued to rejoice, not least of all in his family. Shortly after his father's death, he wrote to his son Johannes, nicknamed Hänschen, congratulating him on progress in his studies and encouraging him to continue to study and pray. He promised his son a present when he came home and wrote to him the story of a beautiful garden full of luscious fruit, toys, and musical instruments. This "heaven" was for boys like Hänschen and his friends who studied and prayed faithfully.

Luther soon learned that his friends in Augsburg were also engaged in diligent study and fervent prayer. Months before, they had prepared, with Luther's help, articles that explained their position on various practical matters of religion. Now, having assessed the situation over against their opponents, they considered these articles insufficient. So Melanchthon went to work drafting new articles emphasizing that the Lutheran position was orthodox, that is, in line with the teachings of the ancient church, and supportive of civil government, not radical or revolutionary. Melanchthon gave the Lutheran understanding of justification by faith, that is, the idea that human good works played no role in salvation, a central position and addressed differences between the Lutherans and the Roman Church but without the extremes of polemic that often characterized the theological works of the time. He simply did not address some sharply disputed points, such as the nature of papal authority. Luther reacted positively to this draft. The Lutheran princes presented the final version of the document, which came to be known as the Augsburg Confession, to the emperor on June 25. After reading Melanchthon's text, Luther wrote to him that he had conceded "more than enough" to the papists. In response to reports that Melanchthon was anxious and despairing over the outcome of the diet, he acknowledged his own physical and spiritual suffering, describing them as the work of demons, concluding, "One has to suffer if he wants to possess Christ." But he considered Melanchthon's despair particularly pernicious, since he seemed to have lost his trust in God. He reminded Melanchthon once again that the matter was in God's hands, chiding him, "The end and the outcome of this cause torture you because you cannot comprehend them." Luther continued in this vein when he wrote to Spalatin the next day. Luther called the fierce opposition the Lutherans encountered at the diet a "good sign," believing it confirmed that they were in the right and that God was fighting for them. He continued to tweak Melanchthon, adding that God "is powerful to do beyond whatever we ask and understand, even though Philip thinks and wishes that God should work in the frame of and according to Philip's own counsel." Luther wrote to Melanchthon again at the beginning of July after rereading the Augsburg Confession. "I am tremendously pleased with it," he said. Yet Luther also criticized some points in the confession; later on he argued with Melanchthon over concessions he had made to the authority of Roman bishops.

At the beginning of July, however, all were wondering how the emperor would respond. He had shown indications of generosity, in contrast with his brother, Archduke Ferdinand. Luther reported, "It is astonishing how all are filled with affection and applause for the Emperor. Perhaps, by God's will, as the first emperor was a very bad one, so this last will be a very good one." By "the first emperor" Luther meant Charles at Worms, suggesting that he might have had a change of heart in the decade intervening between that diet and the one at Augsburg. Even when Luther heard that Charles planned to force a return to former church practices until a general council could convene, he ascribed this strategy to the papists surrounding the emperor rather than to the emperor himself. Charles had, in fact, commissioned the Catholic theologians to prepare a document refuting the Augsburg Confession. On August 3 the emperor had the resulting Confutation read to the diet as his answer to the Lutherans' position. Subsequent attempts to negotiate a compromise—negotiations that Luther thoroughly deplored—came to nothing. By the end of September the diet, voting against its evangelical members, decreed that reform should await the decision of a general council, Catholics were free to practice their religion in any territory, and the publication of evangelical writings should cease. The Protestants had until the following April to reconsider their position.

The theological answer to the emperor's decision came from the pen of Philipp Melanchthon in the form of the Apology (Defense) of the Augsburg Confession. The political answer was the formation of a defensive alliance uniting the Lutheran princes. In October, some of the Wittenberg theologians, including

Luther, met with the elector's lawyers. They discussed once more the legitimacy of resisting the emperor. Finally, Luther and the others allowed that such resistance might be justified under imperial law. The lawyers had argued that the law of the empire permitted resistance to authority in clear cases of injustice. Luther was not entirely convinced by this approach and continued to declare that a Christian should never violently resist the authorities. In this case involving the princes and the emperor, however, he was apparently somewhat relieved to allow the lawyers to have the last word. The way was cleared for a defensive alliance, and the Schmalkaldic League, named for the city of Schmalkalden, where the agreement was to be finalized, was formed. The league's members pledged to come to one another's defense should the emperor attack, and each pledged substantial numbers of troops to the endeavor.

The Religious Peace of Nuremberg (1532)

Following the Diet of Augsburg and the formation of the Schmalkaldic League, the Lutherans found themselves in a dangerous but not yet hopeless situation. The emperor wished to dismantle their reforms and threatened to do so forcibly. Yet few in the empire were eager for war. Luther himself had not expected the Diet of Augsburg to come to an agreement on the religious questions, but he had hoped for a political peace. Once the results from Augsburg became widely known—the final printed edition of the diet's decisions did not reach Wittenberg until March 1531—Luther published a treatise he had composed months earlier titled *A Warning to His Dear German People*. The *Warning* concerned a possible declaration of war by the emperor. Luther reiterated his belief that the emperor himself did not desire this course of action but added that such a war would be unjust, and he called on all the German people, not just his followers, to refuse to fight. Luther's publication caused an outcry from his ardent opponent Duke George of Saxony, who claimed it violated the diet's ban on evangelical publication. The emperor's April deadline for evangelical compliance with Augsburg came and went in the midst of negotiations between his representatives and the Lutheran princes. Halley's comet appeared in August 1531. Luther did not hesitate to interpret such signs for rhetorical effect, even though he put little stock in them personally. He said the comet predicted difficult times for Charles and Ferdinand.

At about the same time, Henry VIII was trying to obtain an annulment of his marriage to Catherine of Aragon, who had failed to produce a male heir for him, so that he could marry Anne Boleyn. The pope refused to annul the marriage, not least because of pressure from Catherine's nephew, Charles V. Henry then looked for opinions from universities throughout Europe, including Wittenberg, that would contradict the papal ruling. He sent Robert Barnes, who had studied at Wittenberg several years earlier, to solicit favorable opinions from Luther and Melanchthon. Philip of Hesse also spoke to the Wittenberg professors in favor of Henry's case, hoping that England could be won for the Schmalkaldic League. In this case, however, Luther agreed with the pope. But he also thought it would be better for Henry to have two wives rather than to divorce Catherine. Later on Luther would give similar advice to Philip of Hesse and have cause to regret it.

In the midst of such international political considerations, both the emperor and the Lutherans more eagerly sought a peaceful settlement of their differences, and negotiations toward that end began in earnest in March 1532. By July they had agreed to disagree about religious matters until a general council of the church or a national assembly could meet. In the meantime, the Lutheran princes assured the emperor they would help in case of war against the Turks. Several weeks after this religious peace—or "religious standstill," as some would call it—of Nuremberg, Elector John died and was succeeded by his son, John Frederick. Luther preached the funeral sermon, as he had done seven years earlier for Elector Frederick. The funeral was held early on a Sunday morning. Luther looked down from the pulpit of the Castle Church and told the gathered mourners that it was no sin to be saddened by the elector's death but that this death should also remind them that Christ died for their salvation. Luther went on to say that the elector had "died" a more terrifying death in the preceding years when he had to endure harsh and violent opposition to the confession he had made at Augsburg. "This is the real, horrible death," Luther stated, "when the devil wears a man down." He was speaking, of course, from his own experience of despair (*Anfechtungen*) but also speaking for many others in that congregation who had gone through desperate times at the diet and in the subsequent negotiations. The preacher left unstated a wish that now perhaps the Wittenbergers could enjoy a more tranquil existence under the new elector, John Frederick.

Against the Anabaptists

Although Luther continued to preach and write against the Roman church in the 1530s and 1540s, he spent as much or more time attacking those he labeled "enthusiasts and Anabaptists." Beginning already in 1524, individuals who moved beyond or apart from Luther or Zwingli in their teaching and practice emerged from the Reformation ranks. Many, in opposition to the universal practice of infant baptism, taught that only adults ready to live an obviously Christian life should be baptized and for this reason were called Anabaptists. Others focused on the imminent return of Christ in judgment resulting in the call for believers to separate themselves from church and society. Some like Thomas Müntzer, as we have seen, involved themselves in the Peasants' War, while others attempted a more peaceful advance of what historians have called the Radical Reformation.

Michael Sattler, for example, had attempted a peaceable consolidation of Swiss Anabaptist groups. Sattler, a former priest converted by evangelical preaching, had traveled throughout Switzerland and southwest Germany spreading Anabaptist teaching. In 1527 he orchestrated a gathering of Anabaptist leaders for the purpose of providing unity within the movement. The Schleitheim Confession of Faith, the points of agreement that emerged from this meeting, reflects issues of general concern to Anabaptist groups. The Confession articulates their rejection of infant baptism and of most practices associated with the Roman church. The articles also express their general wish, over against reformers like Zwingli and Luther, to separate from society, along with their particular opposition to capital punishment and warfare, taking oaths, and allowing Christians to serve in government. This desire to be separate from the rest of society brought the wrath of most governments down upon Anabaptist heads. To reject infant baptism was to reject incorporation into the community. To refuse to fight, hold office, and take oaths (a necessity for business at the time) was to reject the responsibilities of citizenship.

With Anabaptists already under a cloud of suspicion for their beliefs, their story took a tragic turn in the city of Münster. In 1534 the rapidly growing Anabaptist congregation there attracted the attention of Anabaptist leaders more radical than Sattler. One of these, Jan Matthijs, who was preaching in Amsterdam, identified Münster as the "New Jerusalem," God's chosen city that would survive the coming divine judgment, which he had predicted would take place at Easter. As a result, Anabaptists streamed into Münster from other areas. The bishop of Münster, feeling threatened by this gathering, enlisted the aid of the Lutheran prince Philip of Hesse for possible armed intervention. The citizens of Münster also began to arm themselves, departing from a generally pacificist stance with the encouragement of Matthijs. When the bishop moved to lay siege to the city, Mathijs arrived and assumed leadership, eventually expelling from the city all who were not Anabaptists. A charismatic leader, Mathijs nevertheless suffered a blow to his credibility when Easter 1534 proved not to be the end of the world as he had predicted. In an attempt to rally the Münsterites, he led an attack against the besieging forces but was killed. John of Leiden assumed leadership inside the city and led the gathered Anabaptists into even more radical beliefs and practices. He enforced a communal use of all goods and allowed men to have multiple wives. Eventually he declared Münster a kingdom with himself as king. The siege continued until the city was taken in June 1535. John of Leiden and other leaders were executed; their adherents scattered, and their version of Anabaptism quickly disappeared.

Münster confirmed the worst fears that both Catholics and Lutherans had harbored about Anabaptists. The survival of a peaceful form of Anabaptism required the remarkable leadership of Menno Simons. A former Catholic priest, Simons regrouped the Anabaptists scattered by the Münster debacle through his writing and preaching. He strenuously rejected any who continued to promote militant or revolutionary ideas. The Mennonites, the most prominent modern heirs of Anabaptism, are named for Menno Simons.

Preaching in Wittenberg

Luther had preached only rarely in Wittenberg in the months before he left for Coburg. He was disillusioned because his preaching seemed to have had so little effect, so he refused to preach until the people's behavior improved. His boycott of the City Church pulpit ended with his return from Coburg Castle. He resumed his usual Sunday sermons and also took over for Pastor Bugenhagen during his frequent travels. As a result, Luther often preached twice on Sunday and two or

Photo 5.1   Luther in the pulpit by Lucas Cranach. A detail from the lower part of the group of paintings surrounding the altar of the city church in Wittenberg. Source: Stiftung Luthergedenkstatten in Sachsen-Anhalt

three times during the week. His sermons lasted from thirty minutes to an hour, depending on the occasion. (Some preachers, like Bugenhagen, went on much longer than this.) Luther's heavy preaching load came in addition to his other duties and was often interrupted by his own travels and by illness. By 1532 he was exhausted. When Bugenhagen returned, Luther ceased much of his preaching in the City Church and very often would preach only in his home.

When Luther did preach, either in his home or in the church, he could speak beautifully and powerfully about salvation through faith in Christ. On some occasions, however, he showed that he remained unimpressed with the behavior of his fellow citizens. He had always had a negative view of human nature, believing that even Christians fell into sinful behavior rather easily. In a 1522 Christmas sermon he talked about how people always think that had they been in Bethlehem, they would have helped Mary and Joseph. Yet these same people refuse to help the poor who live among them. "It is a plain lie and deception for you to think you would have done a lot of good for Christ, if you do not do it for these people," Luther concluded. "Had you been at Bethlehem, you would have paid just as little attention to him as did the others." Later in his life he frequently railed against greed and stinginess, excoriating people for exploiting rather than helping their neighbors. He also preached against immoral sexual relationships and quite frequently about drunkenness, which he considered a particularly German vice. In one sermon from 1539 he lamented, "Where one can find sermons which will stop the Germans from swilling I do not know." He surmised that the Turks were able to go to war successfully because they did not drink, whereas "when the time comes for us to defend ourselves and be prepared, we get drunk." The princes who should limit such behavior were, according to the preacher, the worst offenders. "Germany," Luther concluded, "is a land of hogs and a filthy people which debauches its body and its life. If you were going to paint it, you would have to paint a pig."

Luther's frustration with moral conditions in Wittenberg mounted once again, until in July 1545 he sent a letter to Kate announcing that he did not plan to return from a trip he had taken. "I would like to arrange matters in such a way that I do not have to return to Wittenberg," he wrote. "My heart has become cold, so that I do not like to be there any longer." He suggested that Kate move to a farm they owned outside of Wittenberg. He was concerned, among other things, that the citizens of Wittenberg would make life difficult for her after he died. "The Word of God is being mocked," he exclaimed. "Away from this Sodom!" He thought that the Wittenbergers had destroyed his "hard and faithful work." Luther's announcement shocked his university colleagues, and they asked the elector to intervene with the recalcitrant reformer. The elector dispatched a personal letter in the care of his physician, who eventually persuaded Luther to come back to Wittenberg.

Health and Home

From the end of 1524 on, Luther was frequently ill. His complaints likely resulted from a combination of stress, the self-inflicted privations of his life as a monk, and old age. He suffered from dizziness, fainting spells, ringing in the ears, and kidney stones. Several times he reported that he could not finish preaching because he was dizzy. Physical suffering triggered Luther's spiritual suffering (*Anfechtungen*), and he believed that faith in Christ was the appropriate remedy for both kinds of suffering. At any rate, he had little faith in physicians and complained bitterly about some of the cures they forced on him during his various illnesses. His symptoms became so severe that on numerous occasions he believed that he was about to die. While Luther was in Schmalkald in 1537, for example, he suffered incredibly from kidney stones. He grew so sick and weak that he was sent back to Wittenberg in a cart, presumably to die at home. Although every effort was made to keep the patient comfortable, the jolting of the cart on the rutted road caused Luther excruciating pain. But the jolting also caused the stones to pass, and he ultimately recovered from this illness.

That Luther should have wished to return home was self-evident. Despite his harsh words about Wittenberg, he had created a home for himself there. His family life was happy and comfortable, if not quite as idyllic as it is sometimes depicted. He and Katherine complemented each other in their activities and interests, but it took them some time to appreciate this. She proved an excellent manager of their large household. She had always cared for and tried to improve their house, the former Augustinian monastery. When Elector John gave them this "Black Cloister" free and clear in 1532 as a reward for Luther's service, Katherine set about rebuilding it in earnest. She also acquired property, particularly for gardens, and became something of a part-time farmer. Martin, who tended to disapprove of her real estate purchases, sometimes referred to her farms and gardens when he addressed her in writing. In one letter he called her "the lady at the new pig market," after a large garden they owned outside the Wittenberg city wall. In another she was the "wealthy lady at Zölsdorf," a rundown farm that she had bought in order to keep it in the Von Bora family. Although Luther appreciated Katherine's household efforts, especially the well-appointed table she laid for his guests and the beer she brewed, he was not always fully aware of how much these things cost. In addition, and much to Katherine's exasperation, he was generous to a fault when he met someone in need. He parted willingly with whatever cash they had on hand and, if they had none, would give away silver dishes instead. Eventually Katherine managed to temper Martin's excessive generosity.

Luther wrote and spoke frequently about marriage. He valued marriage highly and, as we have seen, believed that the Roman church had been wrong to require priests to be celibate. His attitudes toward the relationship between husband and wife were, in many ways, traditional. He often celebrated married sexuality, but he did not think that sex between married couples could occur entirely without sin. Following Augustine, he believed that sexual passion resulted from sin. Luther also accepted without question the husband's superior position in home and society. "The wife governs the household," he said, "preserving without damage, however, the husband's right and jurisdiction. The dominion of women from the beginning of the world has never produced any good."

The household Katherine managed was quite large. The Luthers had six children—Hans, Elizabeth, Magdalena, Martin, Paul, and Margarete. Elizabeth died as an infant, and Magdalena died when she was thirteen. Her death was a particular blow to her parents, who had treasured this daughter born after her sister Elizabeth had died. Family members in residence at the Black Cloister also included Katherine's aunt, Magdalena, and a number of Martin's nieces and nephews. The household also comprised servants, university students who boarded with the Luthers, and very often guests from out of town. When Prince

George of Anhalt planned to stay with Luther on a visit to Wittenberg, the prince's friends advised against it. The Luther household, they said, was noisy and crowded—far from the peaceful refuge you might expect a famous theologian to inhabit.

When Luther preached in his home, as he frequently did later in life, he faced a sizable congregation. Likewise, when he sat down at the dinner table, he had a large and appreciative audience—university colleagues and friends in addition to members of the household. Soon some of the guests began to take notes, recording Luther's more memorable statements. This "Table Talk" offers a glimpse into Luther's everyday life and how he looked at the world around him. It also provides some of his more controversial statements and should be read with some care, or at least not too seriously. For example, Luther's tongue was firmly in his cheek when he said, "When I die I want to be a ghost and pester the bishops, priests, and godless monks so that they have more trouble with a dead Luther than they could have had before with a thousand living ones." At times Luther reminisced, for example, about his trip to Rome in 1510. "I wouldn't take one thousand florins for not having seen Rome," he stated, "because I wouldn't have been able to believe such things if I had been told by somebody without having seen then for myself. We were simply laughed at because we were such pious monks." At other times he spoke freely about others, including his colleagues and even the elector. Melanchthon came in for criticism at Luther's table because of his belief in astrology. "He's very much deluded," Luther said, "for he's easily affected by signs in the sky and he's deceived by his own thoughts. He has often been mistaken, but he can't be dissuaded. Some time ago when I came from Torgau feeling quite weak, he said that I was fated to die then." Luther could praise and blame at the same time, as when he talked about Elector John Frederick. "He is the right man for the job. He is cutting down on his drinking." Luther frequently took lawyers as the target of his verbal jabs, because of or despite the fact that members of the law faculty were frequent guests at his table. At one dinner he said, "If I had a hundred sons I wouldn't bring up one of them to be a lawyer." His son Hans, of course, later studied law.

Although Luther could be very critical of the citizens of Wittenberg, he did have friends among them. One of these was Peter Beskendorf, known as Peter the barber. Peter once asked Luther to give him a simple way to pray. Luther responded with a booklet based on the Lord's Prayer, the Ten Commandments, and the Creed. He emphasized thoughtful prayer and meditation on these texts, cautioning Peter against a mechanical repetition of words in prayer. Luther also encouraged him to concentrate on his prayers and not allow his mind to wander. "A good and attentive barber," he wrote, "keeps his thoughts, attention, and eyes on the razor and hair and does not forget how far he has gotten with his shaving and cutting. If he wants to engage in too much conversation or let his mind wander or look somewhere else he is likely to cut his customer's mouth, nose, or even his throat. How much more does prayer call of concentration and singleness of heart if it is to be a good prayer!" Luther wrote this booklet early in 1535, and it was printed four times that year. On the Saturday before Easter 1535, Peter the barber stabbed his son-in-law to death. The family had been gathered for dinner. The son-in-law, who was a soldier, boasted that he had survived in battle because he could make himself impervious to any wound. The drunken Peter decided to test this boast and stabbed his son-in-law in the chest. The wound was mortal. Peter was arrested and avoided execution only because Luther and others intervened with the court. Peter was exiled from Wittenberg. That Luther should defend someone guilty of such a crime does not mean that he lacked moral standards but testifies rather to his belief in the power of sin and the frailty of human nature.

University Life and Lectures

The University of Wittenberg continued to attract students from throughout Europe. The university clearly led the way in Protestant theology and was engaged in higher learning more generally as well. For example, the faculty discussed Copernicus's idea that the sun was the center of the universe as early as 1539. Luther did not accept this revolutionary theory, believing it contradicted the Bible. Melanchthon, too, was skeptical but for different reasons. Nevertheless, other Wittenberg professors were more enthusiastic. One of them, Joachim Rheticus, who had been a student of Copernicus, encouraged his teacher to publish his findings and then arranged for the posthumous publication of *On the Revolutions of the Heavenly Spheres*.

Whatever Copernicus said about the sun, Luther remained the star at the University of Wittenberg. Melanchthon might have surpassed him in sheer erudition, but Luther was the ranking theologian. In 1535 he became dean and held the office for the rest of his life. He did not allow the deanship to burden him unduly and involved himself very little in the actual administration of the university. He continued to write and to lecture—by this time lecturing only when he wished on any topic he chose. Only Melanchthon among the professors enjoyed this same privilege. The preferential treatment accorded Luther could, however, reach embarrassing levels. His son Hans was allowed to begin university studies at the age of seven and received his bachelor's degree six years later. Some students did attend university at that age, but in this case it probably had less to do with Hans's ability than with his father's status.

As always, Luther remained immersed in the Bible. He preached even in the classroom, and the lectures he gave later in his life read more like sermons than lectures. This is not entirely due to our changed expectations of what a sermon or lecture should be—the lectures he gave later in life are more animated and less pedantic than his own earlier efforts. Luther's lectures on Galatians, delivered in 1531, offer a perfect example of his later style. When he introduced the book, he explained the argument the apostle Paul made in terms of the distinction between the passive righteousness of Christ that is able to save and the active righteousness of humans that is not. As a pastor might explain it to a parishioner, Luther told his students that Christians who are troubled by their sin are tempted to look at their own failed attempts at righteousness rather than trusting solely in the righteousness of Christ. Faced with that temptation, the Christian should forget the active righteousness altogether and think only about the passive righteousness.

Luther encouraged his students to practice this art so that they could also apply it to others. In addition to this pastoral focus to the lectures, Luther did not hesitate to apply Paul's letter to the Galatians to the religious controversies of his day. Luther's opponents, including the pope and the radical reformers, were equated with those who opposed Paul's gospel in the first century.

An image created by Cranach, the "Allegory of Law and Grace," depicted visually what Luther had spoken in the classroom. On one side, the terrors of the law are depicted. God sits in heaven as judge with Moses holding the tables of the law in the foreground. The devil and death use a spear to prod a naked man toward the fires of hell. On the other side, John the Baptist points a man toward the crucified Christ. Blood from Christ's wounds sprinkles the man who also sees Christ rising from the grave. Cranach produced the image as both woodcut and panel painting, and it was frequently copied. This is only one of the more famous examples of how art and imagery continued to spread the Reformation message.

In June 1535 Luther turned his attention to the first book of the Bible, Genesis, planning to lecture on it until he died. He probably did not expect to lecture on this book for almost eleven years, but even then he did not finish it. The Genesis lectures are practically a compendium of Luther's mature theology. Through them he managed to impart everything he believed necessary in theology to the future pastors who sat before him taking notes. In this way the "poor, old preacher," as Luther styled himself in a tract addressed to the Wittenberg students, formed a generation of Lutheran preachers.

The Controversy with Agricola

Although Luther believed that the gospel miraculously united the Wittenberg movement, there were divisions within the Lutheran ranks. Luther's controversy with Johann Agricola affected him deeply and personally. Agricola began his association with Luther in 1516 as a student at the University of Wittenberg. He witnessed the Leipzig debate and Luther's burning of the papal bull. When Agricola completed his studies, he preached in Wittenberg and lectured at the university. Luther treated Agricola as a valued colleague, and he became a favorite preacher at the Saxon court. In this capacity he was part of the delegation to the two Diets of Speyer and to the Diet of Augsburg. By that time he was working in Eisleben, although not always happily. The difficulty of his situation led him to misunderstand Luther's 1536 request to be involved in the Schmalkald negotiations as a job offer. Agricola immediately packed up and moved his family to Wittenberg. Because there was no employment for him, they lived for some time in the Luther house.

Luther put Agricola to work preaching but was surprised by what he heard about his colleague's sermons. Agricola was preaching that God's law played no role in the Christian's life. That sounds similar to what Luther himself had said but was not quite the same. Luther believed that God's law was not a means of salvation but needed to be preached to Christians so that they would recognize their sin and repent. Agricola rejected even this role for the law. What Agricola preached was, in fact, the same opinion that had brought him into conflict with

Melanchthon almost a decade earlier. At that time Luther had been able to smooth over the differences. Now, however, Luther attacked Agricola in disputations and with a pamphlet and helped to restrict Agricola's preaching. Luther began to regard him as someone in the mold of Thomas Müntzer—a former student who had became a radical leader of the Peasants' War.

Agricola might have clung stubbornly to a misapprehension concerning Luther's theology but he was no Müntzer. In 1540 Agricola eagerly accepted the job of court preacher to Elector Joachim II of Brandenburg in Berlin as a way out of Wittenberg. Joachim, wanting to maintain good relations with Luther and preserve the reputation of his territory, helped to manage a settlement between Luther and Agricola that included the retraction of his errors. Although Agricola still considered Luther his mentor and teacher, Luther felt deeply wounded by what he perceived as Agricola's defection from his teaching and continued to warn others about his former student. Luther could forgive moral failings far more readily than he could doctrinal errors. The former were often, according to him, momentary lapses in judgment, while the latter represented conscious decisions that could have eternal consequences.

The Wittenberg Concord

While the controversy with Agricola emerged, another was put to rest, at least for the moment. The Marburg colloquy had highlighted differences concerning the Lord's Supper between Swiss and southern German Protestants on one side and Luther and the northern German theologians on the other. From the time of the Diet of Augsburg, Martin Bucer, the reformer of Strasbourg, worked to overcome this division by demonstrating that the south Germans taught in accord with Luther. Toward this end, Bucer had negotiated a compromise with Zwingli, who was killed at the battle of Kappel shortly thereafter. Bucer then persuaded the southern Germans to accept the Augsburg Confession, something they had not done at the diet.

In May 1536 Bucer and a delegation of theologians from southern Germany arrived in Wittenberg. The formula they signed satisfied Luther and his colleagues that there was sufficient agreement on the nature of Christ's presence in the sacrament for them to be in fellowship. Although the Concord was very Lutheran in tone, it did not require precise definition on some of the contested points. For example, they all agreed that Christ's body and blood were present in the sacrament. The question for the southern Germans had always been what role faith played in this presence. Did someone who did not believe receive Christ? The Wittenberg theologians would have answered yes, because Christ's presence depended on his promise rather than on anyone's faith. The southern Germans could not quite believe that Christ would give himself in this way to people who did not believe. In the end, both sides agreed to state that Christ was *offered* even to those who were unworthy without pressing the point of what the unworthy actually *received*.

The Wittenberg Concord demonstrated that the Protestant movement had not fragmented completely or irretrievably. Moreover, it reveals that Luther was capable of compromise in his old age. He did not insist on some definitions that he knew Bucer and his colleagues could not accept. Although not every Protestant city accepted the Concord, it did pave the way for a continued influence of Lutheran ideas on Protestantism.

Called to a Council

Pietro Paolo Vergerio, the pope's representative to Germany, visited Wittenberg in November 1535. A year earlier the new pope, Paul III, had decided to convene a general council. His predecessor, Clement VII, had successfully delayed in meeting the emperor's demand for a council to decide the religious issues that threatened to tear apart his empire. The popes in general had been wary of councils and avoided convening them whenever possible ever since the papacy struggled with conciliarism—the idea that a council's authority was superior to the pope's—in the fifteenth century. Pope Paul III, however, was one of the sixteenth-century popes who took the reform of church abuses seriously, although that did not necessarily make him friendlier toward Luther than other popes had been. This pope's fear of what unchecked abuses would mean for the church was greater than his fear of a council. The pope's nuncio, Vergerio, traveled throughout Germany to begin discussions about the proposed council. When he visited Wittenberg, he invited Luther to meet with him.

On November 7 Vergerio and Luther met for breakfast. The reformer dressed carefully for his meeting with the nuncio. He had himself shaved and put on his best clothes, including a fur-lined coat, along with a number of gold rings in order to look as youthful as possible. Bugenhagen went with him, and although they could have walked quite easily, they took a carriage to the gates of the city. Luther's conversation with Vergerio began with the topic of Henry VIII, whose representative was in Wittenberg at the time and had refused to meet with Vergerio. Luther commented on the anger the nuncio expressed against the English monarch, who had taken control of the English church and executed two high-ranking officials who opposed him, Cardinal John Fisher and Thomas More. Luther seems to have gone out of his way to further annoy Vergerio by speaking German more often than Latin throughout their conversation. When their talk turned at last to the topic of the council, Luther agreed that the Roman church badly needed one but the evangelicals did not. When Vergerio expressed his belief that a council would decide against the Lutherans, Luther countered that he was so confident in his teaching, he would attend a council even if it meant his death. The meeting ended without either man convincing the other. More than a decade later, however, Vergerio, increasingly frustrated by church abuses and under suspicion by the Venetian inquisition, became a Protestant.

Luther succeeded in presenting a vigorous appearance to Vergerio, but he was really in poor health. Knowing that Luther might not have long to live, Elector John Frederick wanted him to write a definitive statement of faith that his followers could use at the coming council. The elector stipulated that Luther's statement include articles about the papacy. In light of the pope's call for a council, the Lutherans could not pass by the issue of papal authority as they had at Augsburg. Luther's *Schmalkald Articles* articulated his theology in a straightforward and entirely unapologetic fashion. After discussion and some editing by the other prominent Wittenberg theologians, they were to serve the Schmalkaldic League's preparations for a council. To that end the league met at Schmalkalden in February 1537. The members of the league agreed to reject a summon to the council because it would be controlled by the pope and so did not meet their demand for a truly free council. They did not agree to use Luther's articles as a formal statement of faith. Instead the Augsburg Confession would continue to function in that way along with a statement specifically concerning papal authority written by Melanchthon. That statement offered no compromise with the pope but simply codified the anti-papal stance of the Lutherans.

Luther left Schmalkalden before the meeting had concluded because of his near-fatal attack of kidney stones. Once he had recovered in Wittenberg, he continued his work in light of the call for a council. By 1538 he had begun what was to become a massive treatise on the church, *On the Councils and the Church*. Here Luther marshalled the forces of church history to demonstrate his conviction that neither councils nor fathers could be considered authoritative for the Christian faith. Scripture alone remained his authority. "Put them all together, both fathers and councils," he wrote, "and you still will not be able to cull from them all the teachings of the Christian faith, even if you culled forever. If it had not been for Holy Scripture, the church, had it depended on the councils and fathers, would not have lasted long." Convening a council, according to Luther, was a tactic the pope used only when he found it convenient to shore up his authority, and even then the promised council might not be delivered. At the beginning of the treatise, he compared the call for a council to a joke played on a dog: "I often joined in the general laughter when I saw someone offer a morsel of bread on the tip of a knife to dogs and then, as they snapped at it, slap their snouts with the knife handle, so that the poor dogs not only lost the bread but also had to suffer pain. That is a good joke." But not, Luther concluded, when the pope plays this "dog's joke on Christendom" by holding out the hope of a council only to delay continually in actually calling it. This would, in fact, be the case once again—a general council would not be convened until 1545 in the city of Trent.

Luther maintained a strongly anti-papal position for the rest of his days. One of his last works, published in 1545, was titled *On the Papacy at Rome, an Institution of the Devil*. His vehemence, however, stemmed not from his own treatment at the hands of the pope but from his theological position. The papacy, he believed, had undermined the true faith of Christ's apostles and had redefined the church as a human rather than divine institution. The papacy had preached works instead of grace as the means of salvation, and for that reason alone could be condemned as diabolical. Luther and his followers believed that they had restored true Christian teaching as presented in the ancient creeds of the church. Believing they were the true church, they resisted convening their own council to counter the one called for by the pope because they believed such a council would appear merely competitive and schismatic. It was difficult to put such high standards into practice at all times, and as others took hold of Luther's ideas, even to advance and defend them, his own theological understanding was easily misunderstood, obscured, or ignored.

The Bigamy of Philip of Hesse

Philip of Hesse had defended Luther and his theology without entirely under-standing either one. So it is not surprising that when Philip wanted a different wife, he made Luther complicit in one of the stranger incidents of the Lutheran Reformation. Philip's marriage, like all marriages involving the nobility at that time, had been arranged for political reasons. He did not feel well-matched to his wife, and so, like many other noblemen, he found other sexual partners. Philip's philandering, however, troubled his conscience to the point that he rarely received communion, even though he was one of the leading advocates for Luther's reform. Philip believed the solution for this problem was to marry a woman he truly loved. But to do that he would either need to have his first marriage annulled, divorce his wife, or commit bigamy. An annulment could be given only by the pope, who was unlikely to help Philip out of his dilemma. A divorce would not be accepted by Luther, who adhered strictly to the biblical mandates against the practice. Finally, Luther himself counseled bigamy—with dire consequences.

Philip of Hesse married a second wife in December 1539 with the understanding between him and those who advised him, including Luther, that the marriage should not be made public. His new wife's mother did not adhere to that provision, and soon the quiet second marriage became an open scandal. The marriage threatened Philip's position as Landgrave of Hesse and through him the entire Schmalkaldic League. Bigamy was illegal in the empire and could provide Charles V a reason to declare Philip deposed. A few years later, Philip's bigamy would be one of the justifications for the emperor's war against Hesse and Saxony.

Historians have concluded that Luther's advice to Philip to marry a second wife was one of the worst mistakes he ever made, and Luther himself would have agreed. Yet at the time he believed that he was acting as a pastoral counselor to Philip. Luther always saw the second marriage as the least objectionable of several bad choices. He believed that life often forced people into situations where none of the remaining choices was free of sin. People were sinful and could never fully imagine the results of choices they had to make. In such cases, Luther would advise people to "sin boldly," as he put it in a letter to Melanchthon, because he would also advise them to trust in Christ even more boldly. Christians did not have to be sinless—that was an impossibility—but they had to be faithful. So in the case of Philip of Hesse, Luther weighed divorce, which was prohibited by the Bible in almost every situation, against bigamy, which had been permitted for the Old Testament patriarchs. So even though Luther did not believe that bigamy should be routinely practiced, it might be considered the lesser of several evils in Philip's situation.

Luther regretted his advice when he understood the extent of Philip's promis-cuity. He had accepted at face value Philip's protestation of pious misgivings about having a concubine and given counsel in that context. Even so, when news of the marriage leaked out, Luther at first told Philip to lie about it. The lie was necessary in order for Philip to protect his land and people, which was a higher good for a ruler than veracity. Moreover, Luther believed that Philip's enemies were in no position to criticize since they lived unchastely themselves. Still he concluded that he should never have advised the course of bigamy for Philip.

He came to see the entire incident as typical of Philip's rash character, although he also believed that it was less important politically than when the landgrave had helped a duke regain his territory against the forces of Archduke Ferdinand several years earlier. "No prudent man," Luther decided, "would have entered upon that course, but overtaken by a frenzy [Philip of Hesse] managed the affair cleverly." He added concerning the bigamy, "Just be calm! It will blow over."

Luther did not dwell on his role in this catastrophe, but Melanchthon, who had served as a witness to Philip of Hesse's second marriage, was greatly troubled by the consequences of the advice the theologians had given the Landgrave. Luther's colleague suffered from a fever brought on by stress. He was unable to hear or speak and seemed to be near death when Luther visited him in Weimar. Luther ministered to his friend with encouraging words and prayers. Melanchthon recovered, and Luther joyfully relayed the news to Katie, concluding, "God, the dear father, listens to our prayers."

The Colloquies

When Melanchthon became ill, he had been on his way to a meeting with representatives of the Roman church that had been arranged by the emperor in an attempt to reach an agreement about religion in the empire. These religious colloquies were held in various cities between 1539 and 1541. Luther did not expect the discussions to achieve anything, not least because he was convinced that Emperor Charles and Archduke Ferdinand would never oppose the pope. Nevertheless, the theologians who participated in the 1541 Regensburg Colloquy, including Melanchthon but not Luther (who remained in Wittenberg) achieved agreement on a statement describing justification. This agreement, however, did not last long. The pope rejected it and a month later the Lutherans were expressing reservations in a reply written by Melanchthon! The problem was that both sides could read their own understanding into the agreed-upon formula. Both Luther and Melanchthon rejected this kind of false agreement. Yet the colloquies were significant because they marked a willingness by at least some on both sides of the religious divide to discuss the differences between them rather than simply to repeat old accusations.

The religious colloquies also marked the beginning of a prominent role in the Protestant Reformation for John Calvin. Calvin had studied law in France as a young man. He became a Protestant while studying at the University of Paris and was forced to flee that city as a result of his advocacy for evangelical teaching. After he left France, he began to write his famous work *The Institutes of the Christian Religion*, intending it originally as a defense of the beliefs of French Protestants, who were being persecuted. He served evangelical churches in Strasbourg and in Geneva, where he would spend most of his career. He had played a role in the introduction of the Reformation to Geneva and then had been expelled when the citizenry balked at the demands of the pastors. When Calvin continued to defend Geneva in writing against Catholic opponents, he was invited to return to the city as leader of its church. By the time he attended the Colloquy of Regensburg, he was just entering into his thorough reform of the Genevan church. In spite of continued opposition, Calvin would create a model church and an academy of higher learning in the Swiss city that would eclipse Wittenberg as the center for Protestant theology. Luther knew little about this younger colleague in reform. Luther had seen the *Institutes* and been generally impressed, although he also noted that he and Calvin disagreed about the Lord's Supper.

In the context of the disappointing results of the colloquies prior to Regensburg, Luther wrote a bitter attack against an old enemy, Duke Henry of Braunschweig-Wolfenbüttel. Henry had tried unsuccessfully for years to keep Protestantism out of his territory and around the time of the colloquies had been responsible for having fires started in several Protestant cities. In the treatise *Against Hanswurst* Luther mercilessly pilloried the Catholic ruler. Hanswurst was a clownish figure in the German celebration of carnival, and Henry had first used the term in one of his writings to describe Elector John Frederick of Saxony. In his response, Luther mocked Henry's writing as nonsensical, attributing it to the clown Hanswurst. Throughout the treatise, which really had the nature of the church as its theme, Luther referred to "arsonist named Harry" and "Harry, the devil of Wolfenbüttel." The verbal war between the two sides escalated and eventually the Schmalkaldic League went to war against Duke Henry, capturing Braunschweig in 1542. Luther considered the victory a gift from God but warned the Lutheran princes not to become proud. For Luther such incidents were never entirely or merely political. He saw everything as an example of either God or the devil at work in the world. Thus Luther's characterization of Duke Henry as a devil was not only polemic but genuinely reflected his judgment on Henry's opposition to the gospel. Luther's use of harsh and violent language, immoderate though it may have been, was most often calculated to serve a specific purpose and has to be read in light of his theological understanding of events.

Luther and the Jews

It is well known that Luther spoke harshly against the Jews and urged their expulsion from Saxony. No excuse can or should be made for his words, but they can be explored in a way that helps to shed light on the difficult situation faced by the Jewish people in medieval and early modern Europe and also on the turbulent currents of the Reformation.

Luther's earliest writings about the Jews were aimed at their conversion to Christianity. In his 1523 treatise *That Jesus Christ Was Born a Jew*, he urged accomodation for Jews within society in order to attract them to the true Christian faith. He also expressed his conviction that the practices of the Roman church had kept the Jews from becoming Christians and that they would believe once they heard the gospel. So the text was directed toward Christian belief and behavior rather than toward the Jews themselves, even though it probably came out of Luther's conversation with a Jew who had converted to Christianity.

Luther's tone was far different two decades later. In 1543 he published *On the Jews and Their Lies*, one of his most infamous treatises. He was replying to a tract attributed to a Jewish author defending his beliefs. Luther had received the tract from a Moravian friend, along with the request that he write a refutation of it.

As a result, the bulk of Luther's treatise is a defense of the Christian reading of the Old Testament, that is, seeing the Hebrew Bible as containing prophecies concerning Christ. He went on to expose lies supposedly told by the Jews about Jesus and Mary. These were all part of the medieval tradition and Luther got them second-hand. Finally, he advised Christian rulers to forbid rabbis to teach, to confiscate Jewish books, to destroy Jewish homes, to burn down the synagogues, and to forbid Jews to lend money.

Many of Luther's contemporaries and not a few of his colleagues criticized him for this treatise. As was often the case, Luther's language was crude and extremely harsh. In addition, this book seemed a radical departure from what he had written twenty years earlier about how the Jews should be treated. Then, he had encouraged people to tolerate them kindly, believing that Jews, like Christians, had been deceived and abused under the papacy. Luther hoped to convert many Jews to Christianity by once again preaching the pure gospel. When that did not happen, he attributed it to Jewish stubbornness—in much the same way he had blamed the people of Wittenberg for not responding to his preaching—and this is one factor in his rejection of the Jews. Thus Luther's reason for opposing the Jews was religious rather than racial. By the end of his life he conceived of them as enemies of the gospel, in the same way he classified papists, Turks, and Anabaptists as enemies of the gospel.

In this case, however, Luther also uncritically received and perpetuated the anti-Jewish ideas of his society. The Jews had been driven out of Spain in his youth and had been expelled from England before that. Where Jews were tolerated, it was only because they lent money to the kings and nobles. As a result, usury, as it was called in the Middle Ages, was often the only trade available to them and made them an object of jealousy in the community. People like Luther assumed that the Jews had chosen this occupation, condemned them for it, and wished to forbid them to practice it. Furthermore, Luther repeated practically every evil story commonly told about the Jews, including those concerning the ritual murder of children, even though earlier he had ascribed these same stories to papal propaganda. The polemics attending the progress of the Reformation also encouraged Luther in his attack on the Jews. Catholic authors frequently charged the Protestants with favoring the Jews and thus suggested that evangelicals were not genuine Christians. In that context, many reformers in addition to Luther expressed an anti-Jewish bias.

Finally, Luther's writing against the Jews cannot be attributed merely to age and ill health. Like his other polemical works, such as that against Duke Henry, the treatise *On the Jews and Their Lies* must be seen as a calculated use of vicious language by Luther in order to defend his cause. The words he wrote reflect an ugly side of his personality.

Luther's Death

In March 1545 Landgrave Philip of Hesse sent Luther a pamphlet printed in Italian that purported to describe the events surrounding Luther's death. Among other supernatural occurrences, it reported that on the day after Luther had been buried, his coffin was empty. Only a sickening, sulfurous smell remained, presumably because Luther had been dragged off to hell. Luther had the pamphlet published along with a note that read in part, "I received this passionate fabrication of my death and have read it most gladly and happily, with the exception of the blasphemy attributing these lies to the Divine Majesty. Otherwise, I don't take it seriously to heart that the devil and his retinue, pope and papists, are so sincerely hostile to me."

Eleven months later Luther would be dead. He had returned to Eisleben, the town of his birth, in order to mediate a dispute involving the Counts of Mansfeld. The negotiations had almost concluded when Luther went to bed after supper one evening and experienced chest pains. He was not surprised that he should die in the city where he was born. The pain continued through the night. Two men standing at his bedside asked, "Reverend father, do you wish to die standing firmly upon Christ and upon his teaching as you have preached it?" Luther's *yes* in answer to that question was the last word he spoke. He died early in the morning on February 18, 1546.

Luther's death marked the end of an era in the history of the Reformation. Two months before he died, the pope had convened a general council in Trent. The Council of Trent, meeting in several separate sessions between 1545 and 1563, would reshape the Catholic Church, responding to the many calls to end abuses although in a very different way than Luther and his colleagues would have wished. A little more than a year after Luther's death, Emperor Charles V stood at his grave. Charles had defeated the forces of Hesse and Electoral Saxony and entered Wittenberg as a conqueror. His triumph, however, was short-lived. The defeat of the imperial forces a few years later resulted in the 1555 Peace of Augsburg. That settlement declared that each ruler in the empire could decide whether his territory would be Lutheran or Catholic and thus opened the way for a Europe that was officially diverse religiously. A year after the peace Charles V abdicated, leaving the empire to Ferdinand, his brother, and Spain to Philip II, his son.

Two days before he died, Luther penned a brief note that would prove to be his last. Its few lines were a meditation on how important experience was for understanding. He wrote that in order to read Virgil correctly, it was necessary to have been a shepherd or farmer; likewise, Cicero could only be understood by one who had served in government. "Let no one think," he continued, "that he has tasted enough of the Holy Scriptures unless he has governed the churches with the prophets for a hundred years." By his own definition, Luther the preacher had not yet tasted enough of the Scriptures to which he had devoted his life. He concluded, "We are beggars. This is true." Even a century of experience could not teach one everything contained in Scripture, so human beings remain beggars before God. Luther died as he had lived—recognizing his desperate need for the grace of God. He died certain that he had found it.

Writing History: Medieval or Modern?

Luther was a product of the late Middle Ages, benefited from early modern humanism, and introduced ideas and emphases new to sixteenth-century society. In pondering the historical significance of Luther's life and thought, historians have frequently asked whether he represents the end of the Middle Ages or the dawning of modernity. In other words, which was the decisive influence on Luther and his theology—the medieval inheritance or the modern impetus?

Wilhelm Dilthey (German philosopher and historian, 1833–1911) claimed that the Reformation in general was a northern European religious expression of the spirit of the Italian Renaissance. He emphasized Luther's battle against the Roman hierarchy as a decisive step in advancing the moral autonomy of human beings. Dilthey saw the Renaissance and Reformation as creating modern ideas of the individual. Ernst Troeltsch (German theologian and philosopher, 1865–1923) argued that the Renaissance could not be identified with modern conceptions of the individual, as Dilthey had done, and that, at any rate, the Reformation was very different from the Renaissance. For Troeltsch, the sixteenth century represented a division in medieval European culture into its constitutive elements—the classical, human element represented by the Renaissance and the Christian, supernatural element represented by the Reformation. Luther, by virtue of concerning himself with Christian theology, stood opposed to the fundamental insights of the Renaissance and could not have been a precursor of modern ideas about the individual. The debate between Dilthey and Troeltsch over Luther's influence hinges on how Renaissance and Reformation are defined and how modernity is understood.

Heiko Oberman (Dutch historian, 1930–2001) continued the discussion at the level of Luther's theology and its relation to his medieval predecessors. According to Oberman, Luther inherited nominalism, humanism, and Augustinianism as a single strand of late medieval thought. Luther benefited from a revival of Augustinian theology that came to him through people like Staupitz. Luther had been taught nominalist theology at Erfurt and modified and expanded its teachings rather than simply rejecting it. Humanist influences reinforced the Augustinian strain in Luther's thought by emphasizing a return to the original sources. Thus, for Oberman, Luther represents a final harvest of medieval theology before the onset of modernity. Other historians, such as Leif Grane (Danish historian, 1928–2000) and Lewis Spitz (American historian, 1922–1999), emphasized the significance of humanist method for Luther's thought. Luther, according to these historians, rejected the major tenets of nominalism. In place of the theological system he had been taught, he embraced the humanist emphasis on return to the sources using original languages in a broader framework of liberal arts education. Luther, if not fully modern, was part of the dawn of modernity rather than a remnant of the Middle Ages.

Such debates represent how historians use specific information about the past to explain broader historical change. Luther's relation to the Middle Ages and modernity is significant because it helps us explore how individuals interact with ideas and events in a specific context to affect the thought and action of others. The question of whether Luther is more medieval or more modern also highlights how historians create and use categories in order to explain and communicate their understanding of the course of history. The terms *modernity* and *the Middle Ages* must be defined and their contents evaluated in order to make a decision about how individuals, like Luther, or movements, like the Reformation, relate to them. What we think about modernity, of course, also has much to do with what we think about ourselves, even in postmodern times.

Luther in His Own Words: Sermon in Castle Pleissenburg

Duke George of Saxony, an implacable foe of the Reformation that had begun in his cousin's territory of Electoral Saxony, died in 1539. His successor embraced the Reformation, and to celebrate he asked Luther to preach in Leipzig's Castle Pleissenburg. Luther took up a topic that occupied much of his thought at the time—the nature of the church.

But what is the dissention between the papists and us? Answer: Over the true Christian church. Should a person then not be obedient to the Christian church? Yes indeed! All believers owe this obedience, for thus Peter commanded in his first epistle, chapter 4. "Thus someone speaks, that what he says he speaks as God's Word." Someone wants to preach, but he wallows in his words and talks about worldly and housekeeping matters. It is always the case here in the church that he should not speak unless he speaks the rich Word of the Householder [of the church, i.e. God]; otherwise it is not the true church. Therefore it should always be known: God speaks. This is how it goes in the world. If a prince wants to rule, his voice must ring out in his land and his house. If it happens thus in this miserable life, how much more should we let God's Word ring out in the church and into eternal life? All subjects and government officials must be obedient to their lord's word—it is called administration. In the same way, a preacher leads God's household by the virtue and power of his office and God's command, and he dares say nothing other than what God has said and commanded. And if someone chatters a great deal about something other than God's word, the church is not in this prattle, even if they shout like fools, "Church! Church! You should listen to the pope and bishops!"

But when they are asked what the church is, what it does and says, they answer: "The church looks to the pope, cardinals, and bishops." That is simply not true! So we must look to Christ and listen to how he describes the true Christian church against all their false shouting. For we should and must believe Christ and the Apostles more than their shouting, so that we speak God's Word and do what St. Paul and, above all, our Lord Christ said: "Where people keep my word, there is my dwelling, there is the builder. My word must remain therein or it will no longer be my house." Our papists want to do better, and so they stand in danger. Christ said, "We will make our dwelling with him," and the Holy Spirit works all of this. There must be a people that loves me and keeps my commandments—in a word, that is what Christ wishes to have.

A Note on the Sources

The following titles are those most likely to be useful to the student wishing to investigate Luther's life more fully. German titles have been listed only in those cases where no English equivalent is available.

Luther's Works

Almost all of the quotations within the body of the text can be found in *Luther's Works*, ed. by Jaroslav Pelikan (Philadelphia: Fortress Press; Saint Louis: Concordia Publishing House, 1955–1986). To help in finding the relevant treatise or lecture, I have used the title for each work under which it appears in *Luther's Works*. Selections from letters or from the table talk can be found in volumes 48–50 and 54, respectively. The selections in each chapter under the heading "Luther in His Own Words" are my own translations from the critical edition of Luther's writings: *D. Martin Luthers Werke: Kritische Gesamtausgabe* (Weimar: Hermann Böhlaus Nachfolger, 1883–).

Biographies

The most complete biography of Luther available is Martin Brecht's three-volume set: *Martin Luther: His Road to Reformation, 1483–1521*; *Martin Luther: Shaping and Defining the Reformation, 1521–1532*; *Martin Luther: The Preservation of the Church, 1532–1546* (Philadelphia: Fortress Press, 1985–1993). A briefer account that emphasizes Luther's theology is James Kittelson, *Luther the Reformer: The Story of the Man and His Career* (Minneapolis: Augsburg Publishing House, 1986). Heiko Oberman, *Luther: Man Between God and the Devil* (New York: Doubleday, 1989) emphasizes the medieval background and the apocalyptic dimension of Luther's thought. Martin Marty's *Martin Luther* (New York: Viking Penguin, 2004) is also helpful. More dated than these but still useful is Roland Bainton's *Here I Stand: A Life of Martin Luther* (Nashville: Abingdon Press, 1978).

The Sixteenth Century

Europe in the Sixteenth Century, H. G. Koenigsberger et al. (New York: Longman, 1968) provides a very good overview of sixteenth-century politics, society, religion, and economy.

For detailed information on sixteenth-century society and economy see *Handbook of European History, 1400–1600: Late Middle Ages, Renaissance, and Reformation*, ed. by Thomas A. Brady, Jr., Heiko A. Oberman, and James D. Tracy (Leiden: E. J. Brill, 1994–1995). Also helpful for the urban Reformation are Bernd Moeller, *Imperial Cities and the Reformation* (Durham, NC: The Labyrinth Press, 1982) and Steven Ozment, *The Reformation in the Cities: The Appeal of Protestantism to Sixteenth-Century Germany and Switzerland* (New Haven: Yale University Press, 1975).

Printing

For more on printing and the Reformation see Elizabeth Eisenstein, *The Printing Press as an Agent of Change: Communications and Cultural Transformation in Early Modern Europe* (Cambridge: Cambridge University Press, 1979) and Mark Edwards, *Printing, Propaganda, and Martin Luther* (Berkeley: University of California Press, 1994). A good source of information on Luther's translation of the Bible is Stephan Füssel, *The Book of Books: The Luther Bible of 1534* (Köln: Taschen, 2003).

Art

Peter Moser, *Lucas Cranach: His Life, His World and His Art* (Bamberg: Babenberg Verlag, 2005) provides an excellent biography of the artist, along with reproductions of many of his works. The relationship between the Renaissance, the Reformation, and art in Germany is the subject of David Price, *Albrecht Dürer's Renaissance: Humanism, Reformation, and the Art of Faith* (Ann Arbor: University of Michigan Press, 2003).

People

The Oxford Encyclopedia of the Reformation, edited by Hans Hillerbrand (New York: Oxford University Press, 1996) is an excellent source for more information on anyone involved in the Reformation and on other select topics.

For more information on Erasmus see Cornelis Augustijn, *Erasmus: His Life, Works, and Influence*, trans. by J. C. Grayson (Toronto: University of Toronto Press, 1991).

For the biography and theology of Johannes von Staupitz see David Steinmetz, *Misericordia Dei: The Theology of Johannes von Staupitz in Its Late Medieval Setting* (Leiden: E. J. Brill, 1968) and by the same author *Luther and Staupitz* (Durham: Duke University Press, 1980).

The only full-length biography of Georg Spalatin is Irmgard Höss, *Georg Spalatin 1484–1545: Ein Leben in der Zeit des Humanismus und der Reformation* (Weimar: Hermann Böhlaus Nachfolger, 1989).

More on Cardinal Cajetan and others may be found in David V. N. Bagchi, *Luther's Earliest Opponents: Catholic Controversialists, 1518–1525* (Minneapolis: Fortress Press, 1991).

Karl Brandi, *The Emperor Charles V: The Growth and Destiny of a Man and of a World-Empire* (New York: Alfred A. Knopf, 1939) and Manuel Fernández Alvarez, *Charles V: Elected Emperor and Hereditary Ruler* (London: Thames and Hudson, 1975) are both useful biographies of the emperor.

On Argula von Grumbach see Peter Matheson, *Argula von Grumbach: A Woman's Voice in the Reformation* (Edinburgh: T. & T. Clark, 1995).

The only scholarly biographies of Katherine von Bora are in German. The most recent is Martin Treu, *Katharina von Bora.* (4th Edition. Wittenberg: Drei Kastanien, 2003). In English, consult the relevant chapter in Roland Bainton, *Women of the Reformation in Germany and Italy* (Minneapolis: Augsburg Publishing House, 1971) or Rudolf and Marilyn Markwald, *Katharina von Bora: A Reformation Life* (St. Louis: Concordia Publishing House, 2002).

Kurt Aland's *Four Reformers: Luther, Melanchthon, Zwingli, Calvin* (Minneapolis: Augsburg Publishing House, 1979) is a good account of the principal Protestant reformers. More on Zwingli can be found in Ulrich Gäbler, *Huldrych Zwingli: His Life and Work* (Philadelphia: Fortress Press, 1986). A good, brief biography of Calvin is T. H. L. Parker, *John Calvin: A Biography* (Philadelphia: Westminster Press, 1975).

Luther and . . .

For a very helpful collection of quotations from Luther on the subjects of women, marriage, and sexuality see *Luther on Women: A Sourcebook*, edited and translated by Susan Karant-Nunn and Merry E. Wiesner-Hanks (New York: Cambridge University Press, 2003).

The most helpful resource on the subject of Luther and the Jews is *Jews, Judaism, and the Reformation in Sixteenth-Century Germany*, edited by Dean Phillip Bell and Stephen G. Burnett (Leiden: Brill, 2006). Luther's polemic against the Jews is treated in the context of all his later treatises by Mark Edwards in *Luther's Last Battles: Politics and Polemics, 1531–46* (Ithaca: Cornell University Press, 1983).

Luther and other reformers, such as Karlstadt and Zwingli, is the subject of Mark Edwards, *Luther and the False Brethren* (Stanford: Stanford University Press, 1975).

Scott Hendrix, *Luther and the Papacy: Stages in a Reformation Conflict* (Philadelphia: Fortress Press, 1981) details the basis for Luther's criticism of the popes.

For those who read German, Helmar Junghans, *Martin Luther und Wittenberg* (München: Koehler & Amelang, 1996) does an outstanding job of situating Luther in that city.

Writing History

More from Erik Erikson and his critics may be found in Erik Erikson, *Young Man Luther: A Study in Psychoanalysis and History* (New York: W. W. Norton & Company, Inc., 1958) and *Psychohistory and Religion: The Case of Young Man Luther*, ed. by Roger A. Johnson (Philadelphia: Fortress Press, 1977).

On Luther's breakthrough see the section titled "The Reformation Discovery" in Bernhard Lohse, *Martin Luther's Theology: Its Historical and Systematic Development* (Minneapolis: Fortress Press, 1999). Marilyn Harran, *Luther on Conversion: The Early Years* (Ithaca: Cornell University Press, 1983) also contains a useful summary of the debate surrounding the dating of Luther's breakthrough in chapter seven.

The various interpretations of the Peasants' War are treated in detail in *The German Peasant War of 1525—New Viewpoints*, edited by Bob Scribner and Gerhard Benecke (London: George Allen & Unwin, 1979). See also Peter Blickle, *The Revolution of 1525: The German Peasants' War from a New Perspective* (Baltimore: The Johns Hopkins University Press, 1977).

Lewis Spitz, *The Reformation: Basic Interpretations* (Lexington, Mass.: Heath, 1972) contains excerpts from Dilthey and Troeltsch. The essential points of the debate between Spitz and Heiko Oberman can be found in their essays in *Luther and the Dawn of the Modern Era* (Leiden: E. J. Brill, 1974).

Chronology

1483	November 10	Martin Luther born in Eisleben
	November 11	Baptized on St. Martin's Day
1492		Columbus's first voyage
1501		Luther enrolls in Erfurt University
1505	January	Luther receives the Master of Arts degree
May		Luther begins the study of law
July 2		In a thunderstorm Luther vows to become a monk
1507	May 2	Luther celebrates his first Mass as a priest
1510		Luther travels to Rome
1511		Luther to teach at Wittenberg
1512	October	Luther awarded doctorate by University of Wittenberg
1513–1515		Luther lectures on Psalms
1514		Albrecht von Hohenzollern elected Archbishop of Mainz
1515		Luther lectures on Romans
1517	October 31	Luther posts his 95 *Theses*
1518	April	Heidelberg disputation
	Summer	Formal legal proceedings against Luther begin in Rome
	September	Luther meets with Cajetan at Augsburg
	October	Papal ambassador Karl von Miltitz to Wittenberg
1519	January	Death of Emperor Maximilian I
	June	Charles I of Spain elected emperor
	July	Leipzig debate
	August	Philip Melanchthon begins to teach at Wittenberg

1520	February	Leo X renews charges against Luther
	June 11	Luther publishes *On the Papacy*
	June 15	Bull *Exsurge Domine* proclaimed in Rome
	October	*Prelude on the Babylonian Captivity of the Church*
	October 23	Emperor Charles V crowned at Aachen
	November	*The Freedom of a Christian*
1521	January	Bull *Decet Romanem Pontificem* excommunicates Luther
	April 17 and 18	Luther appears before the emperor at Worms
	April 1521– March 1522	Luther at Wartburg Castle
1522–1523		Knights' War
1524–1525		Peasants' War
1524		Diet of Nuremberg
1525	May	Death of Elector Frederick
	June 13	Luther marries Katherine von Bora
	December	*The Bondage of the Will*
	December	*German Mass* debuts in Wittenberg
1526	Summer	(First) Diet of Speyer
	August	Battle of Mohács
1527		Visitations begin in Saxony
	May	Imperial troops sack Rome
1529		Luther writes and publishes the catechisms
	Spring	(Second) Diet of Speyer
	August	Peace of Cambrai (between France and Empire)
	September– October	Turkish siege of Vienna
	October	Marburg Colloquy
1530	February	Pope crowns Charles V Holy Roman Emperor
	Summer	Diet of Augsburg
	June 25	Lutheran princes present Augsburg Confession
1531	February	Schmalkaldic League formed
	July	Religious Peace of Nuremberg

1535		Luther becomes dean of theology faculty
	November	Vergerio visits Luther in Wittenberg
1536	May	Wittenberg Concord
1537	February	Schmalkaldic League meets to discuss proposed council
1539–1541		Religious Colloquies in Hagenau, Worms, and Regensburg
1539	December	Philip of Hesse marries a second wife
1542		Schmalkaldic League attacks Henry of Braunschweig
1543		Luther publishes *On the Jews and Their Lies*
1545	July	Luther announces his plan to leave Wittenberg
	December	Council of Trent convened
1546	February 18	Luther dies in Eisleben
1555		Peace of Augsburg
1556		Charles V abdicates

Glossary

Absolution: forgiveness of sins, often the formal announcement of forgiveness connected with confession to a priest.

Allegory: the spiritual (as opposed to literal) interpretation of Scripture generally, or the specific mode of spiritual interpretation that discovers a meaning in the text relating it to Christ or the church.

Anabaptists: general term for sixteenth-century Christians who rejected infant baptism, believing that only adults should be baptized as a sign of their genuine conversion to Christ.

Anfechtungen: German word for temptation. *Anfechtungen* has come to be a technical term in Luther studies that refers to Luther's sense of despair concerning his sinfulness and God's judgment.

Antichrist: an adversary of Christ to arise at the end of the world, according to several New Testament writings. Luther and others applied the term to the pope.

Archbishop: a high-ranking bishop. This rank usually, but not always, results from the importance of his diocese.

Augustinian Order: the Order of Augustinian Hermits, the religious order to which Luther belonged. The Augustinians resulted from a thirteenth-century combination of several smaller monastic orders. The name refers to the fact that they followed a monastic rule attributed to St. Augustine.

Bishop: a church official charged with oversight of churches, priests, religious (i.e., monks and nuns), and lay people in a given geographical area called a diocese. Bishop is a rank superior to priest, and only bishops can perform certain rites, such as confirmation and ordination.

Bull: an official papal decree, so called because of the lead seals (*bulla*) attached to it.

Cardinal: a high-ranking church official. The distinctive mark of the office is the right to vote to elect the pope. Cardinals were frequently used by the popes in diplomacy and administration.

Catechism: originally the texts that were essential to the Christian faith, such as the Apostles' Creed and the Lord's Prayer. The term has come to refer primarily to books that explain those texts, such as Luther's *Small Catechism* and *Large Catechism*, or that teach the Christian faith in general.

Cloister: see Monastery.

Communion: the specific action of receiving the bread and wine in the Mass or Lord's Supper.

Diet: a meeting of the estates—the electors, the princes, and other nobles (including some clergy), and representatives of the free imperial cities—of the Holy Roman Empire. The powers of the diet were poorly defined, and it served primarily to advise the emperor.

Disputation: an academic debate. Disputations could be held in conjunction with earning the doctor's degree, as an academic exercise, or in order to explore a specific topic.

Dominican order: common name for the Order of Preachers, the mendicant order founded by St. Dominic early in the thirteenth century. Many of Luther's early opponents were Dominicans.

Elector: one of the seven nobles who elected the Holy Roman Emperor—the archbishops of Mainz, Trier, and Cologne, the elector of Saxony, the count Palatine, the margrave of Brandenburg, and the king of Bohemia.

Emperor: ruler of the Holy Roman Empire who traced his title to Charlemagne and beyond him to the Roman emperors. Although the boundaries of the empire varied greatly from one century to another, by Luther's day it consisted primarily of what is now Germany.

Evangelical: an early term for those who came to be called Protestants, it is derived from the word *Gospel*. Luther and his followers preferred it to *Lutheran*.

Franciscan order: common name for the Order of Friars Minor, the mendicant order founded by St. Francis of Assisi in the early thirteenth century.

Friar: a member of one of the mendicant orders.

General Council: an assembly representing the entire church. General councils had become important in the late Middle Ages as a vehicle for addressing the papal schism and for reforming the church.

Heretic: one guilty of erroneous teaching in a matter pertaining to faith.

Humanism: a multifaceted intellectual and educational movement of Renaissance Europe. Humanists engaged in studies across a wide variety of disciplines but were especially interested in recovering for use the Greek and Roman classics. Renaissance humanism should not be confused with modern secular humanism.

Indulgence: a remission of the penance imposed as a result of confession. A plenary indulgence remitted all penances imposed but not accomplished. The term also came to mean the piece of paper that granted the indulgence.

Landgrave: a title of nobility used in the Holy Roman Empire to designate a count directly subject to the emperor.

Lord's Prayer: see Our Father.

Lord's Supper: an evangelical name for the sacrament instituted by Christ that Roman Catholics called the Mass. The term *Mass* was still used at times even among Protestants.

Mass: the most common medieval name for the Christian sacrament also called the Lord's Supper or the Eucharist.

Mendicant: a member of a religious order who lives by begging. Certain orders were designated as mendicant, meaning that they (at least originally) rejected large gifts and endowments and instead requested only enough to survive each day.

Monastery: a building or group of buildings set aside as the residence for monks or nuns.

Monk: one who has formally dedicated his life to religious observance. Monks took vows of poverty, chastity, and obedience.

Nominalism: a school of philosophy that originated with William of Ockham. Nominalism centered on the idea that human knowledge is derived from an understanding of individual things rather than coming through preexisting, universal ideas. The term can also mean a particular theological outlook derived from this philosophical approach.

Office: one of the prayer services that was part of the daily routine of monks and priests.

Ordination: the sacrament through which a man becomes a priest. The Lutheran reformers kept ordination without considering it a sacrament.

Our Father: the prayer Jesus taught his disciples, also called the Lord's Prayer. The prayer has always been commonly and frequently used among Christians, and in the Middle Ages it was an important part of lay piety.

Penance: it can refer either to the sacrament in which a priest absolves a penitent of sin or to the specific tasks imposed on the penitent along with the absolution.

Plenary Indulgence: see Indulgence.

Pope: the bishop of Rome and leader of the church in the west. Orthodox Christians in the east did not recognize the pope's claim to universal authority—one of the causes of the schism between the two groups in 1054.

Purgatory: state or place in which Christians who will ultimately go to heaven undergo a final purification before entering paradise.

Relics: physical objects connected with a saint or other holy person. Bones, bits of clothing, or other objects could serve as relics. They were frequently housed in elaborate vessels called reliquaries.

Rule: a monastic code of conduct, often associated with a specific church father or with the founder of a monastic order. Monks were obligated to observe the rule of their order.

Sacraments: ecclesiastical rites believed to bestow God's grace on the recipient; the medieval church recognized seven sacraments (baptism, penance, the Mass, confirmation, marriage, ordination, last rites). Luther believed there were two or three sacraments (baptism, Lord's Supper, confession/absolution) through which God granted forgiveness of sins.

Saint: a holy person, usually one who has been officially recognized as such by the church. According to church teaching, prayer could be directed to the saints but they were not to be worshiped.

Scholastic theology: the approach to theology found in medieval universities. It was characterized by philosophical questions answered by gathering and interpreting authoritative quotations from Scripture, church fathers, councils, and theologians.

Theses: a series of assertions meant to serve as the foundation for a disputation.

Index